See You Soon
Contact with children
looked after by local authorities

Acknowledgements

I am grateful to all the contributors for so generously sharing their ideas with me and then writing them down. Their expertise and concern have been inspiring. I also want to thank Shaila Shah, the Publishing Manager at BAAF and her Editorial Assistant, Susanne Clarke, for their patience and unfailing good humour with an almost incomputerate editor.

Hedi Argent

A note about the editor

Hedi Argent is an independent child care and adoption consultant and trainer. She has been a guardian *ad litem* for 10 years. She has extensive experience of placing children with disabilities and was a founder member of *Parents for Children*.

Hedi has written numerous articles for *Community Care* and BAAF's journal, *Adoption & Fostering*. She is also the editor of *Keeping the Doors Open*, BAAF, 1988 and the author of *Find me a Family*, Souvenir Press, 1983.

See You Soon

Contact with children
looked after by local authorities

Edited by Hedi Argent

B *ritish*

A *gencies*

for **A** *doption*

and **F** *ostering*

Published by
British Agencies for Adoption & Fostering
(BAAF)
Skyline House
200 Union Street
London SE1 0LX

© BAAF 1995

Charity registration 275689

**British Library Cataloguing in Publication
Data**
A catalogue record for this book is available
from the British Library

ISBN 1 873868 30 8

Designed by Andrew Haig & Associates
Typeset by Avon Dataset
Printed by Russell Press (TU)

Contents

Foreword

Remember the
days of old,
understand the years of the many generations.
Ask your father and he will inform you;
your elders and they will tell you.

Deuteronomy, chapter 32.7

This anthology is the result of my own need for such a book.

How and whether to promote contact with children who are separated from their families; when, where, for how long, with whom and for what purpose; these questions preoccupy all child care professionals and dominate planning for children who are looked after by local authorities.

It was not always so. Until the middle of this century, contact, access or keeping in touch were of no importance. At least, they were of no importance to the organisations which cared for the children or the people who worked in them. We do not know what the families and children thought about it. We do know from literature that there was a curiosity about the identity of children like Oliver Twist, but there was no concern about his lack of contact. Even further back, when Moses was found in the bulrushes and adopted by Pharaoh's daughter, no-one suggests that he ought to see his mother who had nursed him for the early months of his life and surely wished him well in his new family. In Deuteronomy, the continuity of the generations and the values of the tribe are given due weight, but it took over two thousand years for children in need to become the subjects of such attention.

In order to make contact plans, in partnership with parents, which will serve the best interests of their children, we have to consider not only what families want and what children need, we also have to learn what contact means to each family, how customs, history and beliefs influence family connections, whether resources can be more ingeniously used and if there is research which can guide us. We must believe, as one contributor forcefully tells us, that quality comes before quantity. The most meticulously planned contact will fail if children and families are not adequately consulted and supported to make the most of it, or if we do not hear or cannot interpret what happens when contact takes place.

Which of the following comments do you prefer? They are written by different workers about the same teenage mother and her baby.

Sandra continues to make unreasonable demands. She tries to see Pearl more often than on the agreed weekly visits. On the one occasion when extra contact was granted, she took Pearl to see her own mother, who has been denied contact because of her mental illness. This shows Sandra's inability to put Pearl's interests first.

Or:

Sandra continues to demonstrate her commitment to Pearl. She repeatedly tries to increase contact, and on one occasion took Pearl to see her own mother, who is not allowed contact because of her previous depressive illness. This may show Sandra's need to provide Pearl with the family connections she missed herself.

It is not only a question of perception and opinion; the first version must surely undermine any attempt to work in partnership with the young mother, who would be aware of the lack of approval even if she did not read it in a report. The careless label of "mental illness" will reinforce the feelings of injustice, suffered especially by women from minority ethnic communities, and will prevent proper exploration of family ties. Two other opposing views were found in the same bundle of reports.

When the mother visits the foster home, she is critical of everything. She changes Pearl's clothes, restyles her hair and insists on bringing food for her. Each contact visit increases the tension between Sandra and foster carer.

When the mother visits Pearl, she strengthens the bond between them by changing her clothes, restyling her hair and bringing food for her. Each contact visit increases the attachment between Sandra and her daughter.

I am sure that readers of this book could find many more examples of how the quality of contact can be viewed in more ways than one. Nor will it escape the reader's notice that practice, as recommended by the professional contributors, rarely matches the experiences described by consu-mers of the professional services. We have a long way to go before families of children who are accommodated, or in care, know that they can rely on support to keep in touch, in a way that feels right to them. The words "challenge" and "difficult" have been much used in this book, but there are no better words to reflect the writers' response to the task ahead.

The task of promoting contact has inherent problems. The families of children who have to be looked after by local authorities are not all resourceful, capable, energetic, reasonable, self-sufficient and punctual; if they were, their children would hardly have to be cared for by strangers in the first place. But if parents have temporarily or permanently given up the struggle, their relief when children are taken away should not be mistaken for rejection. Even if parents have harmed children who require our protection, we do not help those children by devaluing their parents. On the other hand, children who have been abused have already been rendered powerless, and we must not allow our enthusiasm for contact to over-ride their fears and wishes. We have to learn more about the particular importance of siblings for children separated from their families; perhaps only brothers and sisters can bear witness to each other's childhoods. The wider family, friends and neighbours should be included when contact arrangements are made. We have to understand the special needs of children who are disabled. We must be sensitive to cultural, racial and religious differences. We should not overlook the opportunities of working together within our own, and with other organisations. We have to abide by the law and to observe a mass of regulations and guidance. It is indeed challenging to confront all of these issues.

The variety of opinions expressed in the following chapters range from contact at all costs and in all cases to extreme caution in specific circumstances. At the same time, there is general agreement about the need for skilled services to support contact; several writers even make out a case for specialist contact workers. The information and ideas expressed should encourage consideration of many aspects of contact. I hope that multifaceted appraisals, in partnership with parents, will then lead to contact decisions in the best interests of each child.

Hedi Argent
October 1995

1   Contact: An overview

Margaret Adcock

Margaret Adcock is a Social Work Consultant.

Over the last fifty years there have been differing beliefs and policies about the purpose and value of contact between children in care and their families. Changes have been associated with changing ideas about what was happening and what should happen to children who were being cared for away from their families. The pendulum has swung between the need for policies to rescue children from unfit parents and the need to help them return and grow up in their birth families. There has been an increasing awareness that many children will not benefit, and may actually be damaged, by growing up in the care of the state. This has been accompanied by a recognition of the role that contact might play in influencing whether or not children return to their birth families.

Rescuing children from unfit parents

In the nineteenth century, the welfare of children was thought to lie in separation from their unfit parents. The state, through the Poor Law Boards of Guardians, could assume the parental rights of these unfit parents. Until 1945, the boarding out of Poor Law children in foster homes was restricted to orphans or deserted children, or those in respect of whom parental rights had been assumed. Thus there was an association between the assumption of parental rights, separation from unfit parents and boarding out. This boarding out was often a *de facto* adoption. In other words, if the birth parents could not provide proper care for their child, their parental responsibilities were removed and new parents were found to provide permanent alternative care.

Returning children home

The Children Act 1948 changed this position. It laid a new duty on local authorities which was revolutionary in concept and profoundly affected the way in which responsibilities for deprived children were subsequently exercised. Under S.1(3) a local authority was to endeavour to return children wherever possible to their own parents. Permanent separation was no longer to be the preferred method of dealing with deprived children. The right place for most children was to be at home with their birth parents. If a child came into care, the local authorities had a duty to help the birth parents resume their responsibilities.[1]

In the next two decades there was an assumption that most children were coming in and out of care for short periods and that most of them were then returning home. There was no legislation or official guidance about the management of contact at this time. In individual situations, contact might be discouraged because the child was placed a long way from home or because foster parents were unwelcoming and quickly became possessive about the child they were caring for. There were also cases where some forceful parents, who kept up their visiting, were difficult with both their children and their carers and, in some cases, were felt to undermine the placement. There was no research to provide an overall picture of what was actually happening.

The idea of bringing children up in care had very much gone out of fashion. There was comparatively little interest in providing permanence or continuity or in the way in which the agency should carry out its parental role in relation to children in its care.[2]

In 1973, an important piece of research[3] was published which challenged the existing understanding of what was happening. The authors, Rowe and Lambert commented:

'There does not appear to be any general policy of assuming parental rights if natural mothers and fathers lose touch and cease to fulfill any part of the parental role. The overwhelming impression which emerges from the data is that although some overall trends can be observed, there is no well defined or genuinely accepted policy about which children need the protection or control of a court order. There appeared to be a broad division between social service departments which stressed protection for the child and therefore tended to take a somewhat authoritarian line with the parents and those which emphasised a co-operative approach and hesitated to infringe upon the parents' rights over their children. These

positions sometimes appeared even between areas within one authority.'

Rowe and Lambert's research revealed that many children in care were not being rehabilitated with their birth parents and most of these children were felt by their social workers to be in unsuitable placements. Children were experiencing a succession of moves in care and many had lost touch with their families.

The same authors also sharply questioned the nature and efficiency of local authority services for children in care. In a foreword to the book already quoted from above, Roy Parker wrote:

'Children who are in the care of local authorities or voluntary organisations are widely believed to be in a temporary situation pending rehabilitation with their families, or if this is impossible, some kind of permanent alternative such as adoption. This report makes it absolutely clear that neither of these assumptions hold for many children in . . . We have a daunting obligation to decide how best they can be looked after and what plans can be made for them both individually and in terms of the development of guiding policy . . . The interests of the child in long-term care are likely to be best served by a firm commitment on the part of those in a position of responsibility to some *course of deliberate action. It may mean going all out to get the child back to his family – searching out a long-stay foster home or deciding that adoption is the best course. The prospect of striving to take such a firm grip on events may seem to some unfashionably paternalistic or, in the case of adoption, frighteningly final. To others it will appear unrealistically hopeful given the scarcity of social work resources. Either way it will require altering policies and priorities deliberately in favour of children known to be at substantial risk of remaining in care for a long time.'*

Rowe and Lambert's research provoked much discussion and concern. Local authorities had been shown not to be able to be good parents to the children for whom they were responsible. It was clear that efforts needed to be made to prevent the large group of children, identified by Rowe and Lambert, from drifting in long-term care.

Return to a policy of rescuing children

Other events in the early 1970s seemed to emphasise the fact that the best solution for some children might be permanent placement in a new family rather than returning to their parents. The death of six-year-old Maria Colwell in 1973, after she had been returned from a foster home to her birth parents, shocked many people and focused concern very sharply on the rights of children and their need for greater protection against removal from alternative carers and return to their birth parents. There was pressure for legislation which would protect children from both inadequate local authority care and from unfit birth parents.

In the same year, Goldstein, Freud and Solnit[4] published an influential book, *Beyond the Best Interests of the Child*. They argued that although a parent's attachment to a child could bridge quite a lengthy period of separation, a younger child's attachment would be rapidly transferred to whoever was providing for that child's needs. Whoever was providing the day-to-day care of the child would quickly become the psychological parent. The longer the child remained with a substitute parent, the greater that attachment would become and the more detrimental a move back to the birth parent. The implication was that if after separation from an unfit parent a child was then placed and became attached to a new psychological parent, this placement should be given long-term security.

There was, however, vigorous opposition from the British Association of Social Workers, who argued that research evidence suggested that social services were often providing little help to natural parents. In 1974, Thorpe,[5] for example, argued that the social worker has as much if not more to do with the failure of parents as does the lack of parental interest. In the following year, Holman[6] stressed the need for foster parents to offer love without having to regard themselves as the real parents, and for the inclusion of the natural parents in the fostering placement in order to facilitate the rehabilitation of children if that was possible.

Legislation to protect children

The Children Act 1975 (later incorporated into the Child Care Act 1980) made an attempt both to offer some protection for children who had been placed with alternative carers for periods of time, and to prevent hasty action by birth parents. Individual social workers and some local authorities felt that the Act gave them authority to plan and make better provision for permanent substitute care, especially for younger children. Cain,[7] from research on the Children Act, reported that six out of 21 authorities had found the legislation a base from which to promote change, and the provisions of the Act as pegs on which to build these changes.

The influence of the courts in determining contact arrangements in adoption

As some local authorities began to consider placing more children with permanent substitute parents, sometimes for adoption, the question of contact with birth families inevitably arose. The emphasis was on promoting the child's attachment to the new family because this would help to heal past damage and provide the basis for future healthy development.

If adoption was seen as the best way of providing for a child's future, contact had to be terminated because adoption was viewed by the courts as signifying a complete break with the past. There was no concept of continuing contact after adoption. The legal view had a very strong influence on social work decisions about contact and breaking family links. Social workers often felt they had to choose between denying children the legal security of a permanent new family who could meet their needs, and maintaining relationships with birth family members that still had some importance for them.

The legal position was that there would normally be no interference with the discretion of the local authority. It was open to the High Court in wardship to review a local authority decision on access, if there had been impropriety. A local authority might have to satisfy the court that they had properly carried out their statutory duty if they had totally denied access.

It was suggested in a case referred to as *Re AW and EW* that by looking forward to a future possible adoption as a desirable outcome of the case, the local authority had taken into account matters which it ought not to have taken into account. Bridge L. J. disagreed and said:

'The local authority has to look at the overall picture. It has to look at the past, the present and the future when considering what is presently in the interest of these two children, and if one of the possibilities in the future which the local authority sees as a desirable possibility, is the eventual adoption of these children by the foster

parents, I am quite unable to see how it could possibly be said that this was an irrelevant factor and not properly to be taken into account in deciding whether or not it is proper that the mother should have continued access to the children at present.'[8]

Despite this case, White[9] concluded that while the emphasis and line of reasoning may superficially have changed, it seemed unlikely that there would be any real change in practice. He quoted *M v M* in which Wrangham J. said:

> *'I would prefer to call access a basic right of the child rather than a basic right of the parent. That only means this, that no court should deprive a child of access to either parent unless it is wholly satisfied that it is in the interests of that child that access should cease and that is a conclusion at which a court should be extremely slow to arrive.'*

Contact facilitates return to birth parents

Adoption was never seen as the solution for large numbers of children in care. There needed to be other ways of reducing the "drift" in care for so many children. New research in both the UK and the USA began to demonstrate that there was an association between contact and the possibility of rehabilitation back to birth parents from care. It was clear that without parental contact children were unlikely to be discharged from care. Holman[10] found that in his sample of children in foster care, 70 per cent saw mother, and 80 per cent saw father less than once a year or never. Aldgate,[11] looking at children in foster and residential care in Scotland, found that 35 per cent had had no parental contact in the previous year.

If the aim was to return as many children as possible to their parents as quickly as possible, parental contact needed to be encouraged in the majority of cases. In a five-year study in New York, Fanshel and Shinn[12] found that 86 per cent of the parents who were "uniformly high visitors" had their children discharged from care, whereas only 41 per cent of the children whose parents were "uniformly infrequent" in their visiting subsequently went home. By the the end of five years 64 per cent of children had no or minimal visiting. They also found that the amount of casework activity invested explained a significant measure of variance in parental visiting.

The difficulty was to know how to identify those cases where it might be undesirable for the child to return home or where the parent would not be willing to resume care. Dilemmas about whether contact should be terminated often arose from the inability to assess realistically what kind of changes social workers could help parents to achieve in their functioning.

Reunification is, however, dependent on helping parents to resolve the difficulties that led to the child leaving home in the first place. Achieving successful reunification necessitates local authority and social work activity on many fronts. Decisions have to be made, services have to be provided to support and help parents change, children may need direct work, and contact has to be facilitated. Yet the prevailing picture over the last twenty years had been one of drift, passivity and lack of planning. Recognition of the needs of children and families had not been translated into action.

Planning for permanence

At the end of the 1970s, developments in legal and social work practice suggested a new means of avoiding the drift of children in long-term care. The underlying philosophy of the new approach was that young children need and have the right to a stable permanent home and should have the legal security to make this possible. The child in care cannot have a permanent home; permanence can only be achieved if the child has a stable home, either with the birth parents, or, if this was not possible, with adoptive parents.

An integral feature of the new approach was that birth parents were the first resource to be considered in achieving permanence for the child. Parents were to be told about the child's needs and offered help in meeting these within a specified time. They were also to be told that if rehabilitation did not work, the alternative was for the child to be placed for adoption. Demonstration projects in the USA[13] and work undertaken in Lothian in Scotland[14] showed that the numbers of young children (under age eight) in care could be reduced as a result. Many more children returned to their birth parents and others left care to be adopted. A small number of local authorities in England tried to implement this policy for several years.

Should parental contact be terminated?

The question of parental contact then became much more prominent because it seemed that in a number of cases, continuing contact was an obstacle to placing children who could not return home, in permanent new families. At the Association of British Adoption and Fostering Agencies (ABAFA), we became aware of some cases in which apparently damaging parental visits to children were allowed to continue without any real thought having been given to the purpose or consequences of such visits. At the same time, we knew of cases where social workers and foster carers had inappropriately discouraged birth parents from keeping in touch with their children, making it harder or impossible for them to resume care of their children at a later date. Since there was little guidance or discussion of the problem, ABAFA decided to arrange a seminar to examine the issues and subsequently published a book on the subject.[15]

It became clear at the seminar that there was a basic difficulty both in establishing a definition of the problem to be discussed and in deciding appropriate terminology for discussing it. This reflected the range of perceptions among the different professional groups involved. However, the basic issue addressed was whether, and in what circumstances, a parent might or should be prevented from seeing or having personal contact with a child in care.

We had to consider the implications of the concept of contact in its broadest sense. We concluded that the most helpful approach would be to consider the rights of the child to have access to his or her family. In that sense, access might imply actual contact, or simply access to information about the birth family or the ability and freedom to acquire that knowledge. The term access might cover a wide range of varying links which could be made between the child and their family of origin. The nature of the arrangement in any particular case would depend on what was required to satisfy the interests of the child.

We identified the need to consider the purpose of parental contact and its effects upon the overall plan. This idea had apparently not been put forward in any of the previous scant literature on the topic. Clearly a major purpose would be to facilitate the child's return to his or her birth family. If the child was not to return home, he or she would need knowledge of, and/or access to, their birth family and history. The question was, would contact with the birth family make it impossible to meet the child's other needs for security, stability and affection in a permanent alternative family? Was knowledge of the birth family, together with a sense of belonging to a new family and the benefits that flowed from this, more important for some children than actual contact?

Bentovim,[16] a child psychiatrist, presented the potential conflict between a child's need for security and good enough parenting, and the need to ensure that each child had access to their biological family of origin. He pointed out that young children quickly became attached to whoever was caring for them. If a child was removed from "psychological parents" and returned to a biological parent from whom they had become detached, there was a real danger to their emotional stability. Any activity that disturbed the substitute care being given to a child, which might significantly affect the child's already precarious adjustment, should be avoided. If contact with birth parents had such an effect upon the child then termination of such contact might be indicated.

It was also important, however, for a child to have access to his or her own family of origin and to maintain links with the birth family. He quoted the longitudinal study of Fanshel and Shinn[17] who had said that children were more able to accept additional concern and loving parental figures in their lives with all the confusions inherent in such a situation, than to accept the loss of meaningful figures. Fanshel and Shinn had found that visiting by birth parents over a long period of time produced more overt disturbance than in children who were unvisited. But they pointed out that on a number of characteristics, including IQ gains, emotional adjustment and positive assessments by teachers, visited children were better adjusted than those who remained unvisited.

Bentovim concluded that during the early years when security might be greatly undermined, direct contact with birth parents might need to be very limited and then perhaps increased at a later date, when the child's development could extend to encompass a wider view of his or her world. Colon[18] had suggested that, in terms of Piaget's model of development, younger children, preoccupied with concrete modes of thinking, could become confused and find it far more difficult to relate to two sets of parents, than adolescents who are beginning to take a more abstract view of themselves and the world. At a later stage, the greater ability to encompass both the world of extended family and biological family could enable children to understand and gain the greatest benefit from the richness of their inheritance.

Bentovim made a number of important points about the work that needed to be done and the tensions that were inherent in trying to reconcile the two philosophies:
– if the birth parents were to be able to offer their child a helpful experience of contact, they needed to be able to grieve the fact that they could no longer remain parents in the fullest sense of the word and accept the importance of the new carers to the child;
– new carers had to be helped to contain their anxieties that the child might be drawn to the birth family as being ideal and therefore reject them;
– the child, new family and birth family might all need counselling to work through the issues.
These issues had considerable implications for social work resources.

Misunderstandings, misinterpretation and professional inactivity

One of the consistent findings over the last twenty years is that complicated messages from research and professional debates rarely seemed to be understood in their complexity and acted upon in practice. With the exception of a small number of authorities, the planning for permanence philosophy apparently became interpreted as finding new and permanent families for children soon after they came into care. Contact, it was alleged, was terminated in order to facilitate this process. It seemed that little attempt was made to rehabilitate some children with their birth families. In fact, the number of children placed for adoption from care was small and never probably more than about four per cent of the total population of children leaving care. It seems likely, therefore, that access was terminated for some (or many) children who remained in long-term care.

The requirement for a court scrutiny

Pressures for change led to legislation in 1983 which amended the Child Care Act 1980. The new section (12b) imposed a requirement upon local authorities to notify parents, guardians or custodians of access terminations. S.12c gave parents, guardians or custodians whose access had been terminated the right to apply, within six months of the termination notice, for an access order from a juvenile court. Any order made could specify the commencement, duration, location or any other relevant detail about access. Separated parents and foster carers or others with whom the child had lived for at least six weeks within the last six months were to be notified of any hearing and could make representations to the court. The child could be made a party to the proceedings, although he or she could not initiate an application for access, and a guardian *ad litem* could be appointed on their behalf.

Millham et al[19] commented that the legislation represented something of a compromise, being a considerable curtailment of social workers' power, but restricted in scope to terminations of parental access, so leaving other access arrangements to professional judgement. Millham suggested that there was a growing awareness, however, that in determining the best interests of the child, relations with the birth family had to be carefully considered.

The code of practice – identifying the purpose of access
S.12g of the new legislation required the Secretary of State to prepare a code of practice on access to children in care to be laid before Parliament.[20] This was published in 1983. It did not have statutory authority but had significance, both as a guide to good practice for social workers and as an evidentiary factor in legal proceedings. The code of practice offered more explicit guidance about the principles and management of contact than anything that had hitherto been stated by the Government. It described the need to relate contact to the plan for the child and the management and practice necessary to facilitate access. It also identified the circumstances in which termination of access might be required.

The value and purpose of access in the care plan should be clearly understood and agreed by all concerned
Paragraph 7 emphasised the need to identify the purpose of contact and to link this to the plan for the child.
   *'When a child is admitted to care, the local authority must reach a
   clear decision quickly on the short-term plan for the child and a*

longer term plan where necessary. Consideration of access is an essential element in this process. There should be a firm agreement from the outset about the arrangements and what is expected from the local authority and the child's parents in connection with the arrangements.'

Facilitating and sustaining links

The code of practice said:

> *'There will be no doubt that children's interests will be best served by efforts to sustain links with their natural families.'*

Paragraph 3 stressed the need for access arrangements aimed at reuniting the child with the family if that can be achieved.

> *'Where a child comes into care under Section 2 of the Child Care Act 1980 (voluntary care) there is a specific duty to seek to return the child to his parents or to a relative or friend, providing that is consistent with his welfare. And for the majority of children, however they come into care, the aim from the outset will be to reunite the family if that can be achieved. Promoting and maintaining close links between parent and child are essential to this objective. It follows that local authorities have a positive responsibility to promote and sustain access.'*

Terminating access

Paragraph 4 spelled out the circumstances in which access might *not* be in the child's best interest.

> *'This may happen because there are clear indications that access is damaging to the child or because it must be recognised that there is no realistic hope of rehabilitation and the child's future lies with a permanent substitute family. The local authority may conclude that termination of access is an essential part of such a plan for a child.'*

Involving birth parents and foster carers

Other sections of the code dealt with the details of good practice in achieving these aims. All decisions about access needed to be explained to parents and discussed with them and confirmed in writing. Planning was more likely to be succesful if parents – and others connected with the care of the child – were involved from the beginning in assessment, reviews and decision making. Local authorities were required to place a child near his or her home as far as practicable (Paragraph 19). Foster carers' abilities to promote successful access and rehabilitation depended on the recruitment, training and support which were available. Foster carers needed preparation and continuing support to help them to cope with problems which might accompany contact. Birth parents also needed help to cope with the stress of seeing their child in someone else's home, and living as part of someone else's family. Parents should not be left to make their own way to a placement for the first time and introduce themselves to the foster carers. Ideally, the social worker should bring the birth parents to meet the foster carers before the placement was made (Paragraph 21). Similar provisions should be made for residential care staff (Paragraph 23). Parents might need advice and help with travelling arrangements. Local authorities had power under Section 26 of the Child Care Act 1980 to help with costs (Paragraph 27).

Although parents now had some legislative remedies to enable them to appeal against local authority decisions, there was dissatisfaction from the outset about the way the new arrangements were working. Many local authorities seemed to make little attempt to implement the code of practice, so that initial arrangements and the management of contact did not reflect the guidance contained in the code.

More research findings – the pressure for new legislation

A large body of research findings published by the Department of Health and Social Security in 1985 fuelled the discontent about the nature and quality of social work planning, care experiences, contact and services for rehabilitation offered to children and families. The Department's overview of the research, *Social Work Decisions in Child Care,*[21] identified a number of areas of dissatisfaction.

The care experience

It was said that far less attention was given to what was to happen after admission to care than to whether or not to admit. If children stayed long in care, social work attention faded. The Dartington project had concluded that their findings

'... *highlighted with considerable precision a situation that had long been known – that unless a child left care quickly, that is within six weeks, he or she has a very strong chance of being in care in two years' time. Yet the administrative arrangements within social services and social work practice often do not reflect this acutely short time scale ... Once a child has come into care and the earlier pressure from other agencies and individuals to admit no longer applies, there is a consequent relaxation in the priority accorded to the case by the social worker as attention shifts to more pressing cases.'*[22]

Discharge or remaining in care was not usually the result of social work planning.

'*In general the process of leaving care was not accorded much attention by most social workers. Remaining in care is not always the outcome of a decision but may be the outcome of not taking a decision. Many children remained in care or in a particular placement not as the result of an explicit decision that would be the best course of action – but by default.'*[23]

Family links were seldom given much consideration
As a result, circumstantial barriers to access might go unrecognised and little practical help was offered to encourage parents' visits. When links withered, chances of the child's return home were diminished.

In the Dartington cohort, only 36 per cent of families had specific restrictions imposed on their access but 66 per cent experienced non-specific barriers of distance, travel problems, rules about visits, or unwelcoming attitudes. At the two-year stage, 41 of 170 children still in care had a mother who did not know their address.

Maintaining links
Difficulties in maintaining links were exacerbated for both children and social workers by the rapidity with which families of children in care changed and reconstituted themselves. At the six-month follow-up,

'*the families of no less than one in seven of children were no longer headed by the same parent figures as they had been six months before.'*

'Many of the family structures underwent radical changes during the child's absence . . . By six months nearly half of the children will have had a major change in their family structure. These oscillations are most noticeable among the families of younger children, a factor which not only prevents their return home and affects their wider relationships but also greatly hinders contact between parents and children.'[24]

Outcomes

Overall outcomes may be quite positive in spite of deficiencies in the care system but evaluation is difficult and for some children the outlook was bleak.

'It was our very strong impression that although many of the placements we studied were working well, they were doing so in spite of the system rather than because of it.'[25]

'If the processes as described in this study characterise all of the local authorities in England and Wales, and there is every indication that they do, then we can conclude that as many as 7,000 out of the 40,000 children who enter care each year . . . are destined for a long stay and withering links with their parents and wider family. It also means that at any one time in state care, at least 18,000 children are without meaningful contact with their parents or wider family, a situation which is likely to impair their functioning and increase their social isolation. Sadly, 7,000 of these children are not only isolated but also do not enjoy a stable alternative care placement and a third of this latter group are likely to be under the age of 11.'[26]

Nevertheless, the research showed that extreme pessimism about care was unwarranted and damaging. The majority of children and parents felt that it had achieved some benefit for them and those who asked for care and were refused were apt to feel bitter, desperate and unhelped. There was strong criticism in the report of the devaluing of parents and relatives and their potential contribution to the care and wellbeing of their children. It was emphasised that there was a need to consult, inform and work with parents.

The DoH report concluded that virtually all social workers appeared to view admission to care very negatively. They saw it as a last resort and as a sign of failing to prevent the break-up of families. The emphasis on whether or not to admit seemed to have got out of focus and drew attention away from consideration of children's needs and how to meet them. *The need for greater clarity about the purposes of care, and for plans and practices to be based on and supportive of these purposes, was a recurring theme coming up in virtually all the studies.*

A new solution? The Children Act 1989

There was general agreement that new solutions must be found and that new legislation was necessary. The provisions of the Children Act 1989 stated that the best place for a child to be brought up, wherever possible, was in their birth family. Local authority care seemed hazardous, if not harmful, as a long-term provision for children.

The provisions of the Act emphasised the need for the following:
- keeping children within their birth families wherever possible;
- reducing the number of children admitted to care through the courts;
- working in partnership with parents;
- providing services for families of children in need to improve the health and development of such children;
- local authorities to promote contact, if children had to leave their birth families, and to return children to their birth families wherever possible.

Detailed government guidance spelt out a system for planning, decision making, contact arrangements, and reviewing, to be undertaken in partnership with parents to prevent drift in care and the weakening of family links. Many more matters were to be referred to the court so that there would be an overview of how local authorities were adhering to the principles of the Act.

Unresolved problems

Despite the history of local authority interventions over the last fifty years, there seems to be an assumption that it will now be possible for nearly all children to remain with their families, or, if they are looked after by the local authority, to return to their birth families within a reasonable period. There is very little awareness in government guidance of the possibility that some children may still stay in care for many years and no detailed advice on how to offer these children and young people a positive care experience over a long period.

The purpose of contact seems to be seen as leading to rehabilitation. Although there is recognition in the legislation that there may be circumstances where it is not reasonably practicable or consistent with the child's welfare to promote contact (Sch 2.S.15.i) the Department of Health guidance does not identify or suggest what these circumstances may be. This means that professionals are left to formulate their own views, to make their own decisions, and to try and convince courts of their rationale.

Future directions

There are still large numbers of children and young people in the care system and it is not known how long some of them will remain. These children have different experiences, different family backgrounds, and different needs. Planning and decision making for them needs to reflect their cultures, racial backgrounds and religion. Contact arrangements need to be related to the individual care plan and must take account of the research findings which show that the problem of maintaining links between absent child and parent is multi-dimensional.

There should be recognition by courts and by all professionals of the complexity of planning contact if birth parents find it hard to resolve their difficulties and/or the time in care lengthens. There ought to be more exploration of the potential conflict, identified by Bentovim, between a child's need for security and good enough parenting, and the need to ensure that each child has access to their biological family of origin. This will not always be an easy task and it will certainly require time, skilled attention, and careful management by professionals.

References

1. Adcock M, White R, and Rowlands O, *The Administrative Parent: A study of the assumption of parental rights and duties*, BAAF, 1983.

2. Rowe J, and Lambert L, *Children who Wait*, ABAA, 1973.

3. See 2 above.

4. Goldstein J, Freud A, Solnit A, *Beyond the Best Interests of the Child*, Free Press, 1973, USA.

5. Thorpe R, 'Mum and Mrs So and So', *Social Work Today*, 6:22, 1974.

6. Holman R, 'The Place of Fostering in Social Work', *British Journal of Social Work*, 5:1, 1975

7. Cain H, 'The Children Act – some wider issues', *Adoption & Fostering*, 5:5, BAAF, 1981.

8. White R, 'Legal issues' in Adcock M, and White R (eds), *Terminating Parental Contact: An exploration of the issues relating to children in care*, BAAF, 1980.

9. See 8 above.

10. See 6 above.

11. Aldgate J, 'Identification of factors which influence length of stay in care', in Triseliotis J (ed), *New Developments in Foster Care and Adoption*, BAAF/Batsford, 1980.

12. Fanshel D, and Shinn E, *Children in Foster Care – A longitudinal study*, Columbia University Press, 1978, USA.

13. Stein T, Gambrill E, and Wiltse K, *Children in Foster Care – Achieving continuity of care*, Praeger, 1978, USA.

14. McKay M, 'Planning for Permanent Placement', *Adoption & Fostering*, 99:1, BAAF, 1980.

15. See 8 above.

16. Bentovim A, 'Psychiatric Issues', in Adcock M, and White R(eds), *Terminating Parental Contact: An exploration of the issues relating to children in care*, BAAF, 1980.

17. See 12 above.

18. Colon F, 'Family Ties and Child Placement', *Family Process*, 17, 1978.

19. Millham S, Bullock R, Hosie K, and Haak M, *Lost in Care : The problems*

of maintaining links between children in care and their families, Gower, 1989.

20. Department of Health and Social Security, *Code of Practice – Access to children in care*, HMSO, 1983.

21. Department of Health and Social Security, *Social Work Decisions in Child Care: Recent research findings and their implications*, Rowe J (ed), 1985.

22. See 19 above.

23. See 19 above.

24. See 19 above.

25. See 19 above.

26. See 19 above.

2 A legal framework for contact

Sandra Graham

Sandra Graham is a barrister in chambers in London specialising in Family Law.

In this chapter I will show that there has been a significant change in the law in respect of contact with a child in care and that there has been a fundamental shift in the philosophy of the childcare legislation as shown in Section 34 in the Children Act 1989.

It should be noted that Section 34 provisions for contact with a child in care are decided in accordance with the general law as laid down in the Children Act 1989, but are separate and different from the provision regulating contact in private law (Section 8, Children Act 1989). This is an order requiring the person with whom the child lives to allow contact, whereas Section 34 describes the order in terms of the contact which is to be allowed between a child and persons referred to in Section 34(1) (a) to (d).

Contact with a child in care pre-Children Act 1989

Prior to the enactment of the Children Act 1989, the court would only be involved in decisions regarding contact where it had jurisdiction to give directions, or the power to commit to care in wardship or following a divorce, or if the local authority was seeking to terminate access. Children in care on care orders, by virtue of the Children and Young Persons Act 1969, had access to their birth family at the discretion of the local authority. There was no opportunity for the birth parent or interested parties to challenge the local authority's plans for access, which could in fact mean no access. From 30 January 1984 part 1A of the Child Care Act 1980 required the local authority to issue a notice of termination of access, if that was the intended plan, and for the notice to be served on the birth parents and other interested parties. By virtue of Section 12C of the Child Care Act 1980 there was the right to appeal against the notice but this only arose when contact had already been terminated. Clearly this was not a full remedy in respect of contact with a child in care, nor an adequate challenge to the local authority's exercise of its discretion.

Further limitation had already been placed upon birth parents and other interested parties. In *A v Liverpool City Council [1981] 2 FLR 222* it was held that '. . . The wardship jurisdiction must not be exercised so as to interfere with the day to day administration by local authorities of that statutory control.'

Clearly the House of Lords had decided that interference with the exercise of the local authority's discretion should be rare. Any intervention would be by way of Judicial Review, meaning that any challenge would present significant difficulties.

Case

The case of *Re: S (a minor)(Access Application) [1991] 1 FLR 161* illustrates how the local authority exercised its power under part 1A of the Child Care Act 1980.

The facts were that the child's mother was a heroin addict and therefore unfit to care for her child. The mother was not married nor did she live with the child's father. The child was placed on the "at risk" register almost immediately after birth. Due to the mother's repeated failures to co-operate with social services under a supervision order, a care order was made, and the child was placed with a short-term foster mother. The child had not lived with the mother since the making of the care order, but there had been periods of informal access. The local authority decided to place the child for adoption. The mother had been sentenced to three years imprisonment on a charge of conspiracy to supply heroin. The local authority decided to terminate access and served notice pursuant to part 1A of the Child Care Act 1980. The mother applied to the juvenile court pursuant to Section 12C of the Child Care Act 1980 for an access order. Her application was supported by the guardian *ad litem*. The juvenile court made an order for monthly access for one hour whilst the mother was in prison, on the basis that there was a realistic prospect of rehabilitation. The local authority appealed to the

Divisional Court of the Family Division. The question on appeal was whether the justices were justified in making such an order, the effect of which was almost certain to impede an effective placement of the child with prospective adopters. The Divisional Court found that the magistrates were "plainly wrong" and allowed the appeal. The mother appealed to the Court of Appeal. The Court of Appeal dismissed the appeal by a majority (Slaughton LJ dissenting).

Justice Butler-Sloss said that she agreed that '. . . the justices were plainly wrong to make an access order when the local authority were actively seeking an adoptive family and where they are not shown to have acted other than responsibly and with the welfare of A in mind . . .'.

The pre-Children Act 1989 legislative framework clearly prevented birth parents and other interested parties from using the court to review the plans and aims of a local authority.

Contact with a child in care post-Children Act 1989
Section 34 Children Act 1989 has introduced major changes in respect of contact with a child in care.

Arrangements for contact with a child looked after by virtue of a voluntary agreement is a matter for negotiation between the local authority, the older child (depending on the child's age and understanding), parents and other persons seeking contact.

For children subject to care orders, Section 34 applies. The operation of Section 34 can be illustrated by one or other of the following examples but this is not an exhaustive list:

i) On an application by the local authority or the child, the court may make such orders as it considers appropriate regarding contact with a child in care (Section 34(2)). For instance, where a child has indicated that his/her stated wish is for there to be increased or reduced contact to the parent or other person.

ii) Applications by persons referred to in Section 34(1)(a) to (d) to increase contact with a child in care (Section 34(3)). Where, for example, there is a care order in respect of a child with face to face contact with the parent or other person and they apply to the court for increased contact.

iii) Or any application by the local authority for leave to terminate contact with a child in care (Section 34(4)), where, for example, the local authority for whatever reason wishes to refuse to allow contact with the parent or other person.

Section 34(1) provides:

'Where a child is in the care of the local authority, the authority shall (subject to the provisions of this Section) allow the child reasonable contact with

(a) his parent;

(b) any guardian of his;

(c) where there was a residence order in force with respect to the child, immediately before the care order was made, the person in whose favour the order was made; and

(d) where, immediately before the care order was made, a person had care of the child by virtue of an order made in the exercise of the High Court's inherent jurisdiction with respect to children, that person.'

It should be noted that schedule 2 part II (children looked after by a local authority) of the Children Act 1989 Section 15(1) provides

'Where a child is being looked after by a local authority, the authority shall, unless it is not reasonably practicable or consistent with his welfare, endeavour to promote contact between the child and (a) his parent, (b) any person who is not a parent of his but has parental responsibility for him, friend or other person connected with him.'

Clearly the Children Act 1989 imposes a duty upon the local authority to promote contact between persons mentioned above and a child in their care which includes taking into account both the child's wishes and feelings according to his age and understanding and the parent's wishes.

Neither the Children Act 1989 nor the schedules thereto define the meaning of "allow" or "promote". The ordinary meaning in the Oxford English Dictionary offers such phrases as "admit of", "help forward", "encourage". Clearly this is of limited assistance, but it can be seen that "allow" and "promote" indicate the expectation that contact should be actively encouraged.

It should be noted that Justice Ewbank in *Re: P (Minors) (Contact with Children in Care) [1993] 2 FLR 15* observed that

> *'Section 34 provides for reasonable access and this should be the norm rather than access at discretion. Reasonable access, of course, is not the same as access at the discretion of the local authority. "Reasonable" implies access which is agreed between the local authority and the parent or, if there is no such agreement, access which is objectively reasonable.'*

The court's powers to make orders concerning contact with a child in care are set out in Sections 34(2), 34(4), 34(5), 34(6) and 34(7) Children Act 1989.

Re: B (a minor)(Care order, Review) [1993] 1 FLR 420 illustrates how the courts have interpreted Section 34 and shows an attempt by the Justices to review the local authority's exercise of its discretion.

Case

The local authority applied to the Family Proceedings Court for a care order in respect of four children. At the conclusion of the case the Chairman of the Justices indicated that they would grant a care order to the local authority with contact to the parents for so long as the children wished. The Chairman indicated that they would review the operation of the care order, progress of the care plan and contact, six months after the date of the order. The order was drawn up reflecting the pronouncement of the Chairman.

The local authority appealed:

Justice Thorpe held that a care order gave the local authority statutory powers and duties which thereafter regulated the management of the life of a child in care. It was the local authority's duty to carry out subsequent reviews at regular intervals as per their duty under the Review of Children's Cases Regulations 1991. It was therefore outside the jurisdication of the justices to seek to review the operation of the Care order in this manner and the appeal was allowed.

This case indicates the very firm and clear view taken by the courts, that the court should not use Section 34 to oversee the correct arrangements within the local authority's care plan. It is possible to re-apply to the court in order to vary contact but S.34(17) prevents a second application within six months of the refusal of an earlier contact application, without the court's leave. In addition, Section 91 (14) allows the court to order that no further application may be made for a particular type of order without the court's leave. The court may use this power to prevent frequent disruptive applications.

Termination of contact

By virtue of Section 34(4) the local authority must apply to the court before it terminates contact with a child in care. There have been a number of cases that illustrate the significant changes that have been brought about by the Children Act in this area of law and the principles that the courts have applied.

Section 34(4) provides:

> 'On an application made by the authority or the child, the court may make an order authorising the authority to refuse to allow contact between the child and any person who is mentioned in paragraph (a) to (d) of subsection (1) and named in the order.'

Where the local authority or the child is of the view that contact with persons laid down in Section 34 (1)(a) to (d) should cease there can be a number of reasons given, such as:

i) contact has become detrimental to the child;

ii) there is no perceived benefit to the child;

iii) the child's own request considered in the light of his age and understanding.

And further, although not normally admitted as a reason in itself, to enable the local authority to plan for permanence unfettered by the limitations of ongoing contacts. This was not the intention of the 1989

Children Act; wherever possible, links with the natural family ought to be maintained alongside plans for permanence.

It should be noted that any application made under Section 34 is a substantive application in which the court is determining questions in respect of the upbringing of the child, and the child's welfare should be the court's paramount consideration. In addition, the child can make this application on his/her own.

In the case of *West Glamorgan County Council v P (No. 2) [1993] 1 FLR 407* Justice Rattee in determining whether a court can make orders incompatible with the local authority's plans under Section 34(4) held that the principle set out in *Re S (a minor) (Access Application) [1991] 1 FLR 161* above, applied equally in cases brought after the enactment of the Children Act 1989. Accordingly, the court ought not to make an order which was incompatible with the local authority's plan for a child, unless the decision of the local authority could be shown to have been made capriciously, or that the court was satisfied upon cogent evidence, that the child's welfare demanded the exercise of the court's power in a manner incompatible with the local authority's plan.

However, in the case of *Re: B (Minors) (Care Contact: Local authority's plan) [1993] 1 FLR 543* Justice Butler-Sloss disagreed with the formation of the test applied by Justice Rattee in respect of Section 34(4). The local authority applied to the County Court for authorisation to refuse contact between the mother and two girls under Section 34(4) in order to be able to place the girls with prospective adopters who were not willing to accept ongoing contact with the mother. The mother opposed the application and asked for increased contact. The Judge authorised the local authority to refuse to allow contact contrary to the recommendation of the guardian *ad litem* who appealed.

Justice Butler-Sloss, allowing the appeal, held

'My judgment (in Re: S *above) recognises the imminence of the new legislation and stated the application of the law as it then stood prior to a statutory presumption of continuing contact. In* West Glamorgan County Council v P (No. 2) [1993] 1 FLR 407, *decided after the 1989 Act came into force, Rattee J followed our decision in* Re: S (above) *and applied an even more stringent test. He did not consider for the purpose of the principle in* Re: S *that there was any significant*

difference between the effect of the pre-Children Act law and the law as it is now.'

'. . . I respectfully agree with his decision on the facts of that, but in the light of the new child care legislation, I disagree with his formulation of the test to be applied . . .'

'. . . Decisions based on Section 22 of the Child Care Act 1980, which has been repealed and not re-enacted may not be equally applicable to applications under Section 34 since the application of the Children Act 1989 to contact is entirely different from the previous legislation. Consequently, the decision of this Court in Re: S *and particularly my judgment must be read with considerable caution. I do not consider that my judgment adapts felicitously into the philosophy of the Children Act. The decision of the court in* Re: S *would not, however have been likely to be any different on the facts.'*

The Learned Judge went on to state that the welfare checklist should be applied and any cessation of contact should be justified but this was not to be seen as 'an open door to reviewing the plans of local authorities.'

The Court of Appeal in the case of *Re: E (a minor) (Care Order: Contact) [1994] 1 FLR 146* made it clear that now the appropriate test to be applied is the test as laid down in *Re: B (minors) (Care Contact: Local authority's plan) [1993] IFLR 543.*

It should be further noted that not only are the courts prevented from reviewing the plans of the local authority, the guardian *ad litem* cannot be retained on a case once a care order has been made so there is no independent review save for Judicial Review in limited ircumstances. In the case of *Kent County Council v C [1993] 1 FLR 308* Justice Ewbank held that the justices had no power to add a direction to a care order that the guardian *ad litem* be allowed to continue with his involvement with the child. This meant that neither the court nor the guardian *ad litem* had any function in the assessment of the rehabilitation programme, including any contact arrangements, once a care order had been granted.

On an application for an interim care order, the local authority made an application for contact between a child and her mother to be terminated. An order was accordingly made that the child was to have no contact with her mother. It was held in *A v M and Walsall Metropolitan Borough Council [1993] 2 FLR 244* by Justice Ewbank, that it was for the Justices to decide whether there should be contact pending the final hearing, and for the court at the final hearing to deal with the question whether rehabilitation had to be ruled out. Pending such a decision, save in circumstances of exceptional and sure risk, contact should be maintained. The Justices had been plainly wrong in coming to a premature decision. It was ordered that there should be reasonable contact between the mother and child but gave leave under Section 34(2) for the local authority to supervise contact if there was damage to the child from the father.

It should be noted that as a matter of urgency, the local authority may refuse to allow contact for up to seven days provided they are satisfied it is necessary to safeguard or promote the child's welfare (see Section 34(6)).

Further, where there is a contact application under Section 34, it is the welfare of the child who is the subject of the proceedings which is paramount, despite the fact that there may be more than one party to the proceedings who is a child. *Birmingham City Council v H (No. 3) [1994] 1 FLR 224*, a case heard in the House of Lords, where both the mother and child were minors but the subject of the proceeding was the mother's child.

Finally, Section 34 should be contrasted with Section 8, "Contact Orders" which means

'an order requiring the person with whom a child lives, or is to live, to allow the child to visit or stay with the person named in the order, or for that person and the child otherwise to have contact with each other,' (Section 8 (1) Children Act 1989).

On examining the case law where contact is opposed by one parent, there has to be cogent and supported evidence to withhold contact and it has been made extremely difficult to refuse contact to the parent with whom the child does not live, by stressing "the right of the child". It should be noted that the local authority is not usually involved in these applications as they are private law proceedings (Section 9 (1) and Section 9 (2) Children Act 1989).

Conclusion

I hope that I have managed to demonstrate by an examination of the case law and the interpretation of Section 34, that there is now a clear opportunity for parents and interested parties to continue to have contact with a child in care. It should not be forgotten that apart from face to face contact there are also provisions for indirect contact by way of exchange of information, letters and presents and even telephone contact, provided the welfare of the child dictates the form of contact. Contact could

'give the child the security of knowing that he is still loved and that his parents remain interested in his welfare and avoid the damaging sense of loss to the child in seeing himself abandoned by his parents. Contact could also enable the child to commit himself to a substitute family with the seal of approval of his natural parents and give the child the necessary sense of family and personal identity. Contact, if maintained, was therefore capable of reinforcing and increasing the chances of success of a permanent placement.' (Re: E (a minor) (Care order Contact) above.)

There is clearly now less opportunity for a local authority to deny contact to children in care and parents have the security of knowing that the courts will closely scrutinise any applications that are made under Section 34.

All professionals involved in the administration of the Children Act 1989 should take this opportunity to truly work in partnership in the best interests of the child involved, in keeping with the philosophy and spirit of the Act to improve the overall circumstances of the children we are here to serve.

Further Reading

1. Hershman and McFarlane, *Children, Law and Practice*, Family Law, Jordan Publishing, 1991 and updated.

2. Clarke Hall & Morrison on Children, (10th edn) Butterworth & Co, 1985 and updated.

3. Department of Health, *The Children Act 1989 Guidance and Regulations Vol. 1,* HMSO, 1991.

4. Department of Health, *The Children Act 1989 Guidance and Regulations Vol. 2*, HMSO, 1991.

5. Department of Health, *The Children Act 1989 Guidance and Regulations Vol. 3*, HMSO 1991.

6. White R, Carr P, and Lowe N, *A Guide to the Children Act 1989,* Butterworth & Co, 1990.

7. Levy A, *Wardship Proceedings*, (2nd edn) Longman, 1987.

3   Systemic and developmental aspects of contact

Caroline Lindsey

Caroline Lindsey is a Consultant Child Psychiatrist and Family Therapist.

Leaving home to go into care – the family in the care system

All families have a story about leaving home. The stories reflect their beliefs about when it is the right time and what the circumstances need to be for the family member to leave. Whilst family members may come and go, sometimes in a state of unresolved conflict with their parents and siblings, there is usually a sense of the family existing over time; a multigenerational family to which people continue to belong even in their absence. The separations come about as a result of maturational processes in the individual family members, influenced by societal and culturally held beliefs about growing up and leaving home.

There are some families whose children have been received into care over several generations. One explanation of this may be that leaving home to go into care has become an accepted way to resolve conflict and the breakdown of relationships in the family. The social services department's role may thus be seen as similar to an "extended family". Nevertheless, when care becomes inevitable, the impact of the separation creates a change in the family of a different order than that of leaving home. It does not come about simply as a result of biological and developmental processes in the individual family member; it is an intervention from outside the family, sometimes against their wishes, forcibly changing their relationships with each other. A decision is made that the parental care needed by the children cannot be provided at home and must be shared with others. This changes the care giving system from one that is biologically based in the private domain, to one that is in the public domain, organised by legislation and provided by non-related adults, either in their own home or in a residential setting. Parental responsibility and parental actions are relocated within a complex family-professional system, consisting of birth parents, foster carers and social workers.

Although the children, depending on age, may play an important part in the decision to go into care, which may be based on their wishes and on their behaviour, ultimately the decision is not made by them. The separation is a loss akin to a bereavement, accompanied by feelings of grief, anger and rejection. It may be experienced as a failure by the parents and children and can be regarded as such by the workers who have attempted to avoid this outcome. There is often also a sense of relief and the kindling of hope for a new start. But by contrast with leaving home, which is a transitional stage in the life cycle of the individual and the family, the removal of a child into care changes the structure of the family. The invisible boundary around the family has been breached and the family will never be the same again.

Being accommodated or in care creates a question about family membership for the child and the family left behind. Whose family do you belong to when you are in care? For some children, especially those who have lived at home during their early and middle childhood, their parents and siblings continue to mean family even when they have been rejected, neglected and abused in that family. There are children whose sense of family relatedness and of loyalty persists in the face of such experiences, making alternative placements very difficult.

Other children have spent years of their lives in foster care and end up not feeling part of the foster family or of their own. Foster families are advised to take great care not to usurp the role of the birth parents by calling themselves foster carers rather than foster parents. Their dilemma is to carry the roles and responsibilities of the family, in particular the provision of security, without being able to offer a lifelong commitment (although many do) and in collaboration with the local authority.

A crucial issue in each case is whether the significance of the parent-child relationship can endure in a meaningful way, when it can no longer be put into practice as parenting. For most children, the relationship will always have significance, but occasionally it may be so destructive that it will be necessary to protect the child and, where appropriate, provide help to recognise and come to terms with the nature of the relationship.

If it is possible for a meaningful relationship to survive, how is this to be achieved? One answer may lie in creating the best conditions for maintaining contact.

The meaning of 'contact'

Since the implementation of the Children Act 1989, professionals in the field of child care and child mental health have grown accustomed to the use of the word "contact" instead of "access". It may be worth considering what impact the change of language has had on workers and on families and to speculate what the intention of the legislators may have been.

It seems to this writer that there is a very fundamental difference between the two words. Access, referring to the access of parents to their children conjures up a parental right to a pathway to their children, rather than the children's right to see their parents. Contact, because of its physical connotation, creates the idea of a mutual experience between parents and children, including the possibility of physical care and intimacy as well as emotional relatedness. The shift from parental rights to parental responsibility underlines the change in attitude to contact – from being the right of the parent to see the child to the acknowledged need of children for continuity in their relationship with their parents. Thus, it becomes the duty of parents and professionals to ensure that contact is not lost. The changes made in the Act reflect changing beliefs and practices about the importance of continuity of relationships in identity formation and the recognition of the adverse effect of the loss of the birth parent on the child's subsequent psychological health.

Contact is not an all or nothing concept. There are infinite variations, each family creating its own pattern. The arrangements for the contact, its nature and frequency carry a message about the relationship along the continuum from 'I will be your parent again' to 'I will always remember you'.

The creation of meaning

The Children Act has provided the framework for the event of contact to take place. Bateson[1] wrote that 'without context, words and actions have no meaning at all'. This idea implies that the meaning given to events such as contact is dependent on the context which creates it. Thus, care and contact, family and parent have different meanings for the child in care than the child at home with the nuclear family.

Social constructionists like Gergen[2] and Pearce and Cronen[3] have taken these ideas further to suggest that the way people give meaning to their experiences is through social interaction, mediated by language. Pearce and Cronen recognised that the way people construct meaning in their lives is through multilayered contexts which may at times be in contradiction with each other. These contradictions account for much of the confusion and conflict which surround such issues as contact. They proposed a model called "The co-ordinated management of meaning" in which they identified six levels of meaning-creating contexts. These contexts inter-relate with each other, so that the meaning arising out of one level of context is affected by another level of context. This happens in a recursive manner.

The "highest" and most general of these contexts is one which arises from the socio-cultural norms of society acknowledged by the individual. These include political ideologies and religious beliefs, educational systems and the legislative framework for the community. In a multi-cultural society such as ours, variations in socio-cultural norms are reflected in the wide range of patterns of family life and family structures which grow out of different ethnic backgrounds. The next level of context is referred to as the family myth. The family derives its sense of identity from its shared images and the stories that portray those images which make up the family mythology over several generations.[4] The context of the life script provides meaning for the individual regarding his or her role. It is built up both from the expectations of the family of origin and the family of procreation, and from the person's life experiences with peers and in education, training and work. Specific relationships between people are contextualised by all the previously described levels. However, as will be familiar from observation, a significant relationship between a couple, man and woman or parent and child, may be capable of transforming all previously held beliefs and attitudes about themselves, thus, in turn, rewriting or editing their life scripts and family myths. Repeated patterns of relating over time, which make up relation-ships, consist of episodes. The episodes themselves are meaning-creating contexts either confirming or challenging prior experiences. Finally, the content of the episodes, both speech and action, what and how things are said and done, the verbal and non-verbal expression of thought and feeling creates meaning in the interaction. This description of the levels of meaning is depicted figuratively in Figure 1 below.

Figure 1
The co-ordinated management of meaning

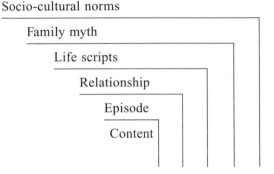

This model can be adapted to provide a conceptual framework for contact and what brings it into being. In this chapter, some specific contexts will be considered which have a particular bearing on the issue of contact.

At the level of socio-cultural norms, important contexts for contact are created by legislation and by how the law is manifested as social services departments' policies. At the level of the life script, the practice of professionals in relation to contact will have been affected by their own life history and training. The ways in which workers carry out their roles in planning and intervening is likely to have been importantly influenced by their understanding of the implications of child care theories and research. Some aspects of research findings, family systems and attachment theories and child development have a direct bearing on contact.

At the level of family myth, at least two sets of families need to be taken into account – the child's birth family and the foster family. Differences in family beliefs about parenting and separation will powerfully affect their ability to maintain contact with each other over time. At the level of relationship, the complex inter-relationships between the child, the birth family, the foster family and the social worker will determine the success of contact by means of the ties of need, love and affection, authority, loyalty and fear of rejection and abuse.

At the level of the episode of contact itself, this includes how, when and where it takes place. The nature of the contact then in turn becomes the context for all the other contexts, influencing relationships, practice and beliefs, ultimately becoming enshrined in societal norms and the law.

The legislative context

As has already been identified, the Children Act 1989 has introduced some important systemic concepts. Access has been replaced by contact and the lineal concept of parental rights has been transformed into parental responsibility which is a relational term. Parents have been empowered by the retention of responsibility under all circumstances except in adoption and by the prominence given to the maintenance of the family system, wherever possible, through partnership and the emphasis on continuity of relationship.

The insistence on hearing the voice of the child gives a place to the child in the system and takes account of the mutually influencing relationship of the child and the parents. It is important in the ascertaining of children's wishes about contact to recognise that what they say they want is to some extent a product of their relationship with the adults in their lives. It is further affected by the fantasy and hope that the parental relationship will be good enough to go back home. As one child put it, it is 'the wish to be ordinary'. Another child realised that his foster carers were unable to support his contact with his parents whom he still wanted to see, despite their previous neglect and inadequacies. These foster carers, in common with many others, found it hard to appreciate what the birth parents had to offer the child because of their incompetence due to their addiction to drugs and alcohol. The child agreed with his foster carers not to see them because he was afraid to lose his new found home. Others agree to see their parents and risk the breakdown of their place-ment which may result from the disturbance created by the contradictory messages – from their parents that they will be coming home and from others that this is not going to happen.

The Act also recognises the damaging effects of physical, sexual and emotional abuse, neglect and rejection on the long-term mental health of children and it acknowledges that there are times when it is more therapeutic for the child to suffer the loss of continuity through total separation.

The social services' context

The social services departments have the responsibility of implementing the legislative framework for contact. Through their policies they articulate the need for children to maintain their family identity whilst at the same time having to achieve a permanent placement. Departments determine the way in which the workers are empowered to carry out this task by their attitude to the provision of support and resources; for example, for the contact work and family finding, adequate remuneration for carers and most importantly, sufficient time and training to do the detailed work required with the child, carers and birth parents.

Influential research findings

It is clear from the review of research findings on the outcome of foster care by John Triseliotis[5] that children who experience consistent parental contact are more stable and settled in their foster care placements. Children who are regularly visited are likely to return home more quickly.

Well being is higher and breakdown rates either the same or lower if children remain in contact with their parents.[6] It is also clear that at least until the implementation of the Children Act, the majority of birth parents were not maintaining contact, especially in permanent placements, and birth parents and foster carers found the contact difficult.[7,8] The positive findings of the research have now been given a legal imperative. This empowers social workers to assess foster carers for their capacity to support contact and obliges them to promote it, despite the inevitable difficulties which may follow.

Family systems, myths, scripts and beliefs

In order to understand the common failure to implement contact, despite its demonstrated beneficial effects, it is necessary to appreciate the

40

conflicts which arise from the differing myths and beliefs of the birth and foster families and from the professionals' scripts about the nature of parenting and family life. These differences fundamentally affect the facilitation of contact. For example, in one case, the middle class, professional foster carers of a teenager who came from a family where violent crime and sexual abuse had occurred, tried to inculcate her with their values. To a great extent they succeeded but at each contact visit, she was drawn back into her family's beliefs which so conflicted with theirs. Her family's story included an admiration for criminal activities and idealised a close relative who had committed murder. This fed into her own rebellious and antisocial behaviour in the foster home. However, the carers persisted with the contact because of the importance of the relationships for her and hoped that she would eventually choose their way of life.

Systems theory
Systems theory[9] provides a theoretical framework for understanding the complex interrelationships within the large system comprising the social services, legal system and the birth and substitute families organised around the child. All these systems are inter-related so that an intervention in one part of the system will have an impact on the other parts. A consultation between the birth parent and social worker concerning contact might change the way the parent relates to the foster carer, which in turn might result in a change in behaviour of the child, without the child being seen. The system is created by the emergence of patterns of relationships over time. This gives rise to rules for family living as well as beliefs about family life which are developed over the generations and are modified with the entrance of new partners from other families. The system also changes as the family moves through the life cycle, requiring changes in the pattern of parenting behaviour. The individuals within the family system are changing and changing the system as they change. Families' beliefs are embedded in the stories they have about their lives and are recreated in their actions.

Whilst each family is unique, I have found it useful to think in terms of a "family of families"[10] in order to draw some distinctions between the experiences of birth, foster and adoptive families, two parent or lone parent families, and divorced, separated or reconstituted families. Recognising that there is a "family of families", rather than a normative family, from which all other systems deviate, validates their varying paths through the life cycle. In particular, it provides a way of thinking about the different ways they come into being, how family life is sustained, how people separate and the meaning of family life for them.

'While she's here, she's our baby, not yours'

Case

This comment was made by a short-term foster carer to Mark, the four-year-old half-sibling of a young baby. Mark's family were hoping to be given a residence order for the baby, because her mother was ill. Both she and they had contact. The foster carer seemed to have no difficulty with the contact of the mother, whom she saw as unable to care for her child. But with the family who clearly would be able to offer the baby a home, she seemed to feel resentful and competitive. The family felt similarly, since they could not understand why the social services would not agree to let them take care of the baby full time before the final hearing. When the foster carer said to Mark, 'while she's here, she's our baby, not yours', in response to a loving gesture made by Mark to the baby, he was devastated. He had been hoping that 'the Judge will let us have the baby' since 'we are such a nice family and we will bring her to see her mother'. He had just begun to appreciate that if this baby was his sibling, then the mother was his mother as well and thus, to recognise his loss.

The foster carer's unconscious, throwaway comment conveys something of the dilemma in which carers are placed. To care well for their foster children means to begin to take them on as their own. Without the attachment, the baby will not flourish; with the attachment, it is hard not to begin to exclude the birth family. So it is easy to see why vulnerable birth parents might stay away. The task of the carers, where there is a possibility of rehabilitation, could usefully be redefined as the foster care of parent/s and child.

Foster family systems need to be open with permeable boundaries so that their ability to parent is not dependent on a belief about having an exclusive relationship with their foster children. Their family story might be one of several generations of caring for the children of relatives and others. Research[11] has shown that successful foster carers are often older, and having completed their own families, are free from the tensions that can arise when the demands of biological and foster children conflict. The foster mother, and sometimes the father, may see their role of carer as a chosen career, as opposed to their role as parents to their birth children. But whether as parent or carer, the family script needs to include a story of accepting children as they are, without a compulsion to impose on them standards and expectations of achievement or ways of communicating and reciprocating affection that do not fit with their life scripts or that of their families of origin. At the same time, they also need a non-judgemental belief in children's capacity to grow and change, within limits and at their own pace, usually very slowly, and to respond to their love and discipline. They require a family script about parenting that values the contribution that different family members make to the process, thus enabling them to accept the birth parents for what they are able to provide rather than seeing them as failures for what they have been unable to do. Their family myth, beliefs and individual scripts about parental and personal authority need to equip them to deal with the children they foster and the collaborative sharing of their role with the social workers, without the loss of their own sense of agency.

In permanent placements, the birth parents have to go through a process of relinquishing their parental role to the carers, becoming "non-parental parents". Yet, they need to retain a belief in their value to the child. This belief will have been undermined by the necessity for the accommodation or reception into care. It will also have been affected by how they were parented themselves and whether family history is being repeated. The significance of the parents for the child, and hence the importance of contact, requires reinforcement from the social worker and the foster carers. If, on the other hand, birth parents are unable to accept that the daily parenting tasks are no longer theirs, they will challenge the right of the carer to look after their child and potentially undermine the placement, creating conflict for the child.

In one case, a mother, who had herself been in care from the age of fourteen years, had never been able to care for her daughter without social work support and respite care, due to her drug dependence. Finally, she had a prison sentence and a decision was made to place her child permanently. She accepted the need for this but wanted to remain in contact with the child, whom she loved and had never rejected, as a friend.

In another case, the parents, after numerous court hearings about their neglect, were unable to accept that their children could not live in the family. The parents saw themselves as providing an important cultural identity from their country of origin and wanted their particular way of life, which had existed over many generations, to be valued by their children. These arguments had been persuasive in the past and several attempts at rehabilitation had been made. However, now even contact seemed impossible, since they repeatedly promised their children that they would get them home, inevitably threatening the security of the placement.

The contribution of attachment theory

John Bowlby[12] coined the phrase a "secure base" to describe the person or persons to whom the child can securely attach. The idea of a "base" arose from the universally observed phenomenon of the young child at play, who runs back to the parent from time to time. Then, the child, having been reassured that all is well and that the parent is there, should the need arise, goes off again. Bowlby proposed that the experience of a secure attachment figure in childhood is essential for psychological wellbeing. The Robertsons[13] investigated the impact of brief separations on normally adjusted children and discovered the anger and distress that they demonstrated on reunion. This work has provided the basis for changes in practice when children are hospitalised or separated for other reasons, insisting on the importance of parents visiting, even if their departure causes temporary pain and is uncomfortable for the carers.

Subsequently, research by Mary Ainsworth[14] using the "strange situation" identified patterns of attachment based on reunion behaviour when young children are separated briefly from their mothers. Three patterns of secure (type B) avoidant (type A) and resistant (type C) attachments were first identified within a sample of normal children. Following this, a pattern of disorganised or avoidant/resistant (type D) attachment has been identified, which is associated with infants with very severely depressed, neglectful or physically abusing parents. Children from such D dyads show inconsistent and contradictory behaviour (such as looking away while being held or approaching with averted gaze), a lack of obvious goals, unusual expressions of negative emotion, and signs of confusion, apprehension and indecision toward the parent. This pattern is very reminiscent of the behaviour of some children described in foster care, who are both avoidant and resistant, clinging and asking for attention and, at the same time, rejecting of the foster carer and unable to respond to affection. The children's patterns of attachment, described by Ainsworth, have been correlated with the quality of the lived and recalled childhood experiences of the mothers. It would be interesting to assess the outcome of contact in relation to the presence or absence of a type D attachment.

Further, it has also been shown that responsive, warm and interactive care is not sufficient.[15] Without continuity of care, albeit not necessarily with only one or two carers, children become attention seeking and unusually friendly with strangers; they become unselective about their relationships. In care, they are at risk of foster breakdowns and more moves as a result. This underlines the need for early decisions about permanent placement and contact, rather than repeated attempts at rehabilitation, which may seem to be according to the letter of the Children Act but are not in the spirit.

It is clear that when the parent–child relationship has been abusive, neglectful or rejecting prior to the child coming into care, there will already be disturbances of attachment. The quality of the attachment, which is now affected further by the separation, will have an impact on any contact which the child has with the parent. Nevertheless, the separation may offer an opportunity for changing the pattern of interaction. Providing that the relationship has not been overwhelmingly damaging, contact will maintain the idea of the relationship, so that all trust is not lost. This will be particularly important if the reason for the separation lies largely outside the parent–child relationship, as happens sometimes, for example, with acute psychiatric illness or addiction, from which the parent may recover. However, failure by the parent to maintain contact is a natural and likely sequel to the insecure pattern of attachment which has been created by the quality of the parenting. It is not surprising that foster carers find it hard to tolerate the continuation of these interactions.

Carers may be confused about how to interpret disturbing behaviour following contact. Understanding, derived from attachment theory, prevents us from attributing it wholly to the quality of the contact itself, although this explanation is regularly given as the reason why contact should be terminated. Attachment theory would propose that the disturbance is also a normal response to the anguish of the separation and the re-evocation of the rejection experienced by the child. Whilst not a reason in itself to stop the visits, the frequent pattern of rejecting and anxiously clinging behaviours, created by the insecure attachment, which are then replayed with the foster carers, may sometimes only gradually cease when the child no longer continues to experience this repetition. Training and support of carers is an essential component in helping them to anticipate and then to tolerate the impact of contact.

Developmental issues

Time

One of the most pressing directions now being made by the courts is for advice about the nature of contact to be ordered. From what has already been said, it will be apparent that the length and frequency of the visits conveys meaning about the future of the relationship and its nature, as well as reflecting the current situation.

Contact arrangements must take account of the changing needs of children as they grow up. Whilst there may be exceptions, the younger the child, the more frequent the contact has to be, bearing in mind the development of the ability to remember. It is important to recognise the different time scale for children and hence, the urgency of setting up review and planning meetings. A year in the life of a two-year-old is half his/her life. All contact meetings should take place in surroundings which allow for spontaneity and privacy, at regular and predictable times.

As children grow older and move into adolescence, the arrangements for contact inevitably have to change. In the first place, adolescents are usually capable at least physically, if not emotionally, of making their way to contact visits. As in divorced and separated families, if the teenager is settled in the foster family, the priority for leisure time may be peer group activities rather than meetings with parents. On the other hand, the young person who has retained meaningful links with the birth family may now increasingly seek contact, sometimes in a quest for information and clarification about the earlier separation or sometimes, in the hope for a rehabilitation. Such steps are clearly best taken alongside consultations between social workers, foster carers and the birth family.

Communication
Communication with young children about their separation from their family and about their wishes for contact is often overlooked because of the concern workers have, that they are unable to tell the child exactly what is going to happen about their future care. This leaves the children in a position of not knowing and also without a sense that these matters can be spoken about. The distress experienced by the separation is then compounded and may manifest itself by an intensification of withdrawal, tantrums and oppositional behaviour or clinging and crying. Even pre-school children can communicate through their play and often in words as well, if they are given the opportunity to do so.

Case
A five-year-old child sat silently crying following the breakdown of her planned permanent placement. Her foster carer said that she had not been able to get through to her, but when we began to use the family figures to describe her own family, it emerged that she had seen herself as her mother's helper with the younger children. Despite the professionals' knowledge of the rejection of this child by her mother, she told us that she thought about her mother every night and worried that her help might still be needed. She longed for contact, which her mother was refusing. We could see that she was not ready for the commitment to a new family. It became clear that her social worker had to try again to persuade her mother to see her, in order to

free her, and that she needed help through therapeutic work to overcome her grief.

Contact with grandparents and siblings

The child's sense of remaining a member of his or her original family can
be significantly enhanced by contact with siblings and grandparents as
well as other relatives. They are often far less threatening for everyone
concerned; contact with them provides a way of maintaining the child's
identity without a competition for parenthood. It may, however, present
a predicament for the grandparents, who may see themselves as having
to choose between their own child and their grandchild. (This issue is
also important when the grandparents are the foster carers and are being
asked not to allow contact or only limited contact with their son or
daughter. This involves denying their child access to their parental home
in order to create security for the grandchild.) The assessment of their
ability to do this is particularly critical in cases where there has been a
denial of abuse.

In the case of siblings, where one child remains in the original home,
the contact, although much wished for, may evoke repeated feelings of
rejection and questioning on the part of the child in care and disquiet
about their different life styles. For the separate foster carers of several
siblings, the effort of sustaining the contact within their busy time
schedules is great and has to be supported by social workers. Again,
problems may be created by the differing expectations and ways of life of
the foster families, resulting in unhelpful comparisons between the
siblings. But on the other hand, contact provides reassurance to the
children about each others' wellbeing, important especially after an
experience of abuse. Even if their needs are such that they are unable to
be cared for in the same family, seeing each other maintains their identity
as brothers and sisters, provided they have lived together previously. It
continues their shared story of the family they came from, providing the
opportunity for their old and new family scripts to be integrated.

Case

In one case, three brothers from a religious community had survived
together through the illness and death of their mother. Their father

was unable to parent them, being neglectful out of ignorance and incompetence. Their emotional needs were so great and their relation ships with each other were so disturbing, that a decision had to be made to separate them. The social services department made a commitment to find foster carers who would be prepared to give priority to the boys' contact with each other – which the children wanted – and with their father, which was more problematic, since they were, to varying degrees, ambivalent about him. Three families were found in another neighbourhood but with the same religious faith. They lived close by each other. The families, whilst having a similar outlook on life, which included a belief in the overriding importance of the blood tie between parent and child, had very different structures and life styles. One couple had been childless, the second family had an older only son and in the third family, there were teenage twins. The foster carers were able to create continuity in many aspects of the children's lives, whilst meeting their individual needs by drawing a boundary around each family, providing security and privacy. This was only achieved by intense social work support, which included assessing and then working with the couples as a group. They subsequently grew into a mutually supportive network.

Summary

Contact is the symbolic representation of the child's relationship with two sets of parents. As such, it can only be created with the help of supporting systems. Birth parents need support to create the story of their ongoing significance to the child. Foster carers need to believe that the birth parents' failure to parent their children does not exclude the possibility that they may still be able to contribute to their wellbeing. To do so, they need to have a story about parenting that does not focus on the nuclear family alone. The social worker needs to be able to strike a balance between the creation of a permanent placement for the child which will not be disrupted, and maintaining the links with the original family. The social worker provides the bridge between the two. This bridge can be reinforced by the use of family consultations where the families can meet psychologically even if not physically, in the process of articulating a new story of family life for and with the child, which includes both families.

References

1. Bateson G, *Mind and Nature: A necessary unity*, Wildwood House,1979.

2. Gergen K, 'The social constructionist movement in modern psychology', *American Psychologist*, 40, 266–75, 1985, USA.

3. Pearce W B, and Cronen V E, *Communication, Action and Meaning: The creation of social realities*, New York: Praeger, 1980, USA.

4. Byng Hall J, *Rewriting Family Scripts: Improvisation and systems change*, London Guildford Press, 1995.

5. Triseliotis J, 'Foster care outcomes: a review of key research findings,' *Adoption & Fostering*, 13:3, BAAF, 1989.

6. Triseliotis J, *Foster Care Outcomes*, Highlight No. 96, National Children's Bureau, 1990.

7. Rowe J, Cain H, Hundleby M, and Keane A, *Long-term Foster Care*, BAAF/ Batsford, 1984.

8. Stratchlyde Social Work Department, *Fostering and Adoption Disruption Research Project: Temporary Placements*, Scottish Office, Central Research Unit Papers, 1988.

9. Von Bertalanffy L, 'The theory of open systems in physics and biology', *Science*, 3, 1950.

10. Lindsey C, 'Family systems reconstructed in the mind of the therapist', *Human Systems*, 4, 1993.

11. Bowlby J, *Separation*, The Hogarth Press, 1973.

12. Berridge D, and Cleaver H, *Foster Home Breakdown*, Blackwell, 1987.

13. Robertson J, and Robertson J, 'Young children in brief separation: A fresh look', *Psychoanalytic Study of the Child*, 26, 1971.

14. Ainsworth M D S, Blehar M C, Waters E, Wall S, *Patterns of Attachment: A psychological study of the strange situation*, Erlbaum, 1978, USA.

15. Tizard B, and Hodges J, 'The effect of early institutional rearing on the development of eight year old children', *Journal of Child Psychology and Psychiatry*, 19, 1979.

4 From access to contact in a local authority setting

Rick Newman

Rick Newman is a social worker in a London Borough.

As a social worker in a local authority setting, and working within a Children and Families Team, it is not uncommon to receive a call from a desperate parent demanding that their child is taken into care. Despite all the publicity which followed the 1989 Children Act, social work with children is invariably seen as concerning "care" and "child protection". Care remains synonymous, in the public mind, with a physical resource such as a children's home or a substitute family. The parents who are requesting the removal of their children usually insist that we find a placement immediately, and a secure one at that. At such times the meanings of "accommodation" or "in care" can be irrelevant and parental responsibility of no concern; all too often parents are moved to add that they know we would have to do something were they to threaten the safety of their child.

It is not surprising that there are confusions in the public mind about social workers and what they do. Many young parents will remember when Care Orders were the norm and when legislation on access, as it was then called, imposed restrictions on parents, almost as though coming to the notice of a local authority immediately rendered them unfit or second class. This remnant of Poor Law thinking marginalised parents whose children were in care, and the children suffered as a consequence. Under the 1989 Children Act the concept of contact has been transformed. A duty has been imposed on local authorities to promote contact for children who are looked after.

A child is "looked after" if they are 'in the local authority's care or provided with accommodation by the local authority' (S.22). Where the arrangement is voluntary the child is "accommodated" and parental responsibility remains with those who hold it already. Only with the coercive powers of a Care Order (S.31), an Interim Care Order (S.38), or an Emergency Protection Order (S.44) does a local authority share in the parental responsibility.

Any application for care proceedings must be made with a detailed Care Plan, identifying the positive reasons for a care order and describing how the care plan will be put into effect. Courts have to be fully satisfied with the course of action proposed and every care plan will be subject to rigorous examination. At the core of each care plan must be the matter of contact: the purpose contact serves, the conditions which might be imposed, whether contact is to be terminated or how contact is to be promoted.

The change from "access" to "contact" is not a change in name only; in practice the change has been enormous. Access was a parental right controlled by the local authority. As a residential social worker fifteen years ago, I remember access as what happened on a Sunday afternoon when children went to visit or were visited. And we like to forget the days when "access" was all too often dependent on the child's behaviour over the previous week, and when "home leave" was more like a military furlough than respect for a child's relationships or an essential component of a plan for rehabilitation.

Under the Children Act, "contact" is endorsed as a child's right, which local authorities are duty bound to promote for all children who are looked after. Only a court now has the power to deny contact, and then there has to be a clear indication that termination of contact would be in the child's best interest.

The Children Act does not stress the difference between children who are "accommodated" or "in care". Where contact is concerned, the differences can be great and to date this has received scant attention in the guidance, only a mention that when children are "in care", it is more likely that contact will have to be supervised. Not only supervision, but aims, frequency and reaching agreements about contact, will probably be affected by how children are looked after. However, the careful planning, regular reviews, commitment and support to ensure quality as well as quantity of contact, will be the same for every child.

The child protection industry
The Dartington Research Unit[1] on access disputes concluded that good

social work practice 'should have nurtured family links because it is to home and neighbourhood most children return on leaving care'. It is suggested that 90 per cent of children who have been looked after by local authorities return home. If this figure is reliable, it highlights the importance of effective contact; however, it is child protection and not contact which claims priority of both concern and resources. With developments such as multi-agency working together, comprehensive assessments, memorandum interviews, protection plans, and manuals of procedures, to say nothing of the tiers of co-ordinators and managers, it is almost as though there is now a child protection industry. All that is needed is a referral to set the machinery in motion in a seemingly impersonal and authoritarian bureaucracy.

The image of child protection practice is such that social work is increasingly viewed as social policing, while parents feel alienated and excluded from the process altogether. Child protection interventions are frequently problem led and essentially reactive in nature. Assessments can all too easily focus on parental weaknesses rather than placing importance on the recognition of parental strengths, or addressing the reasons for any parental failings. Parents frequently complain of feeling powerless in the face of allegations and investigations. It is perhaps not without a hint of irony that a recent Department of Health practice guide is entitled *The Challenge of Partnership in Child Protection.*[2]

The experience of parents and families encountering the child protection industry can have a lasting impact on subsequent arrangements, notably on contact, if their children are then looked after by the local authority. If steps are taken to place a child in substitute care, who is going to remind all concerned of the child's right and the importance of contact? When child protection is a family's gateway to service, local authorities must be able to progress from reactive social policing to proactive work with children and families.

Concurrent with the growth in awareness and understanding of child abuse has been the development over the last decade of management systems in all areas of social care. Local authority managers have had to take account of changing political climates and diminishing resources. The rhetoric of management abounds, and in a local authority setting, the consequences can appear ever more impersonal for workers and clients;

restructuring, targets, performance indicators, cost benefit analysis and workload weighting are everyday facts of life. It is a system increasingly dominated by numbers; though quality is the stated aim, it is convenient to quantify performance. One notes how easily child protection can be reduced to numbers without having to address issues of quality. Quality is difficult to measure. For children who are looked after, contact without quality has no purpose.

The purpose of contact

As most children who have been looked after return home, effective contact is an essential part in any rehabilitation plan. The importance of contact for a child in substitute care is now accepted, but what does it mean for children?

Continuity of relationships
The recognition of the value of a child's existing relationships is in marked contrast to previous assertions that children required a "clean break" from their past. Most children who are looked after are away from their families for only brief periods; substitute care should exist to support and not dismiss existing relationships. Contact should celebrate the child as a member of a family.

Sense of identity
A child looked after is first and foremost an individual, albeit one whose circumstances may necessitate substitute care. Contact is a key means of acknowledging such aspects of a child's identity as race, religion, class and culture.

Validation of the past
Life story work is now widely used as a tool for working with children; contact offers a living history such as 'What was I like when I was a baby, Grandma?' Contact also helps children to understand what has happened, and that they are not somehow to blame for it.

Approval and reassurance
Children need permission to attach or settle into substitute care. They

need to know that their parents approve and they need reassurance about what may be happening in the situation from which they have been removed.

Case

A pair of eight-year-old twins were accommodated at their mother's request when she was hospitalised following a nervous breakdown. The twins were placed with experienced foster carers but became seriously distressed, much to the surprise of all concerned. Contact with their mother was established at the earliest opportunity. As soon as she was helped to visit and to confirm her approval of the placement, the children were reassured that they had not betrayed her. They settled and thrived, which in turn had a positive effect upon their mother's recovery.

Respect for a child's wishes

Children may themselves tell us whom they want to see. To encourage them places value both on contact and on the child's views. Being looked after can all too easily leave children overwhelmed and unheard, despite the emphasis in the Children Act upon ascertaining a child's wishes and feelings.

Case

William is an eleven-year-old boy in care following physical abuse by his father. His mother said William should not continue to have contact with her sister, whom he likes. Despite this aunt's unconventional lifestyle, of which the mother disapproves, there was no reason why William could not see her. William now enjoys regular contact with his aunt and their relationship is appreciated even by William's mother. Being allowed contact with his aunt was one of the first choices William has ever been allowed to make.

Keeping memories alive

If children have no-one who shares their memories, they will fade and be lost. When children can ask 'Do you remember when we . . .' and get a positive response, there is affirmation both of the memory and the relationship. When adults remind a child of 'When you went to the zoo . . .' then memory is treasured. If no-one shares or holds their memories, children experience a heightened sense of loss, isolation and diminished self worth. When children lose their past, they can become trapped in the present, and their future may hold no prospects or attraction.

Preparing for independence

Many children who move to "independence" re-establish family links. If contact is maintained while they are looked after, they may rebuild relationships as young adults which were problematic or disrupted when they were children.

Case

Wayne was accommodated when he was fourteen; his family was devoutly religious and could not accept Wayne's assertion that he was gay. Although Wayne rejected his family and was rejected by his family for several years, and his challenging behaviour resulted in a number of placement changes, contact was maintained on a regular basis. When Wayne moved to his own accommodation, it was with active support from his family with whom he became reconciled. The difficult child had become a much loved young man; contact had prevented an irretrievable breakdown.

Protection and safety

Prescriptive contact can enable a child to feel safe. For example, a child may need to know that alcoholic parents will only be allowed to visit if they are sober; or a child might need the protection of knowing that abusing parents can only send letters via a letterbox service, and agree to have no other contact.

Assessment and observation

Contact can be used to evaluate the strengths and potential in a child's relationships and to monitor developments over a period of time. Assessment and observation are clearly important for agencies, especially if care proceedings are likely, but contact also gives children and their families an opportunity to reassess themselves. With the support of foster carers or social workers, families' relationships can be reordered.

Barriers to contact

There are numerous barriers to contact, but only one is insurmountable:

Legal restrictions

Sanctions as prescribed in a S.34 order, may impose conditions and limits on contact arrangements or, in extreme circumstances, a particular contact may be terminated.

Other barriers to contact arise from a wide range of circumstances:

Scarce resources

In their analysis of barriers to access, Gibson and Parsloe[3] concluded that local authorities did recognise the value of access, but a lack of adequate resources meant that contact was poorly served. Over the past decade and with the implementation of the Children Act, there has been a growth of support services: family centres, contact centres and children's centres, all contribute to the promotion of contact. However, contact can consume massive resources, especially in cases which are complex and contested and when contact has to be supervised.

Social work practice

All too often children come to be looked after in a crisis, and insufficient regard is paid to planning contact. Arrangements tend to emerge and the emergent arrangements become established as the norm. There is also a danger of rationalising as acceptable, unsatisfactory situations which have been allowed to develop at the start of a placement: 'Let him settle for a couple of weeks and then we will look at organising contact' is a frequent comment from a social worker who may be only too relieved to have found the placement. Unallocated cases, or cases being worked by a succession of duty officers, do little for continuity or planning of contact at the crucial early stages.

Social work attitudes to contact

Although contact is now embraced and encouraged in principle, we should recognise that previous attitudes may continue to affect us. Contact has been viewed, in the past, as a child's reward for good behaviour but the Children Act is clear that contact is a child's right, and withdrawal of a child's right to contact is no longer permitted. Attitudes may also mirror a belief that visits to children by their family will cause the child to be disruptive or distressed. Alternatively, there have been assumptions that children who retain relationships might prove unattractive to potential long-term carers. Social workers' belief that children needed a "clean break" from the past, was identified by Berridge and Cleaver[4] as a factor in their study of foster placement breakdowns. Over recent years, there has been considerable research on contact arrangements, but too many social workers remain ignorant of the findings. Local authorities should take positive steps to ensure social workers are aware of trends and developments and that the authority's commitment to contact is reflected in training programmes.

Decision making in isolation
Contact arrangements should be the product of collective agreement rather than a decision made by social workers and imposed on the participants. However, in care proceedings the arrangements for contact are usually the cause of greatest conflict between a local authority and parents, and the negotiated agreement on contact is often a result of last minute "horsetrading" between legal representatives from which both social workers and parents can feel excluded. These negotiations can emphasise quantity at the expense of quality; but if the quality is good, then the right quantity should follow.

Child's wishes
Children's wishes may prove a barrier to contact, and although we should respect a child's wishes and feelings, we may have to consider whether these are in a child's best interests in the long term. We have to keep the door open, to allow for changing views and to discourage children from getting themselves into corners.

Case
    Angela was accommodated at her mother's request following an

incident at home to which the police were called. In her anger, Angela was determined to have nothing to do with her mother and, refusing all contact, she demanded a permanent foster home. Intensive social work input with mother and daughter led to a resumption of contact and an eventual return home.

"Disappearing" parents

Parents may need encouragement to maintain relationships with their absent children. In addition to the "lost" parents described elsewhere in this book, there are those parents who, for whatever reason, might wish to "disappear". It happens that children are accommodated at the request of parents who would prefer to abdicate their parental responsibilities, at least for a time. To sustain the relationship between parents and child can be frustrating and exhausting for social workers. It can also be immensely rewarding.

Parental attitudes
Case

> 'If you have contact with your father, as far as I am concerned, I no longer have a daughter,' said one exasperated mother to her twelve-year-old daughter. The mother refused to see her child or to consider having her home. The social worker did not press the mother to make contact but continued to pass on relevant information, which maintained the mother–daughter relationship until the end of hostilities, when peace could be restored.

Sometimes parents and others demand contact rights which may not be in the child's best interests. If children are separated by the local authority from their families, then some out-of-the-ordinary event has taken place which does not make for smooth relationships. If family dynamics are strained, contact may be used by parents and relatives to test and force children's loyalties. It is then necessary to enable families to meet the child's needs rather than their own.

Impractical placements

Placements often have to be found at short notice and what starts as providing a bed in an emergency, can become an unsuitable setting in which contact is discouraged. Contact can be undermined if the placement is inaccessible or too far away.

Contact and partnership

The concept of partnership is central to the Children Act 1989 and the implications for social work practice are considerable if partnership is to be anything more than good intentions. Local authorities lose few opportunities to remind the general public that we want to work in partnership with them. Partnership suggests consensus, agreement, mutual trust, co-operation and a sense of shared responsibility. However, I prefer to look upon a commitment to partnership with families along the lines of 'We'll try not to stitch you up, but if we do it is not intentional'. Partnership is a means to an end, not an end in itself; it is a relationship and like all relationships it should not be taken for granted.

It is simplistic to view partnership as only concerning the relationship between local authorities and families. For contact arrangements to be successful, there must also be effective partnership between social worker and child, between social worker and family, between social worker and foster carer or contact supervisor, and between social worker and the local authority. Contact can occur without partnership and partnership can exist without contact. However, effective contact is dependent upon effective partnership.

Partnership for parents means their right to be included in making arrangements and plans for their children. It is a right parents may ultimately choose not to exercise or which they may have difficulty in exercising, but it is a right nonetheless and must be respected in practice.

What is best for the child is of paramount importance, but due regard should also be paid to the wishes and feelings of parents. Marsh[5] has identified a role for social workers in partnership as "consultants to the client", with families as the client. Given that social workers can also be called upon to be "servants of the court" and must always act on behalf of the child, the social work task in contact can be difficult, if not impossible, at times.

At crisis point, social workers are preoccupied with finding an appropriate placement and the family from which the child is removed, can be overlooked. There must be jargon-free written information, about what arrangements are being made and who has which rights. Many parents believe they have no rights, even if their child is being accommodated. We must remember that what may be routine for social workers may be a unique experience for parents.

Just as there are barriers to contact, there are also barriers to partnership. Class, race, power, language, past experience of social workers, and parents' sense of failure, can all make partnership precarious. For their part, social workers must believe in the value of partnership and comprehend the implications in order to make the best contact arrangement for the child's sake.

Contact when children are accommodated

The majority of children who are looked after by a local authority are accommodated for a brief period until normal service can be resumed at home. All too often, therefore, contact arrangements for children who are accommodated are taken for granted.

The accommodation of children is a voluntary arrangement between those with parental responsibility and the local authority, a service provided for children deemed to be "in need". A child's right to contact is acknowledged and in theory, and within reason, those with parental responsibility may have contact at any time. However, putting theory into practice requires effort on the part of social workers.

Although the accommodation of children represents an agreement between parents and a local authority, we must not assume that we are automatically working together. Those with parental responsibility should be actively involved in planning accommodation and contact and their views should be treated with respect. Arrangements often have to be made when resources are scarce, time is limited and focused on the here and now. While parents are vulnerable to making agreements which may not be fair to themselves, social workers can make rationalisations to justify a particular placement or the lack of immediate prospects for contact.

Case

Paul's mother, Mary, lived with a violent man who was later diagnosed as schizophrenic. Two-year-old Paul and his mother were assaulted by the man who was subsequently imprisoned for four years. Mary struggled on without family support, with mounting debts and Paul's increasingly disturbed behaviour. In her despair, Mary asked for Paul to be accommodated in April 1993 and to be adopted. Daily contact was established between mother and son but rehabilitation work soon proved unproductive. In June 1993, the local authority adoption panel agreed that Paul should be adopted; contact was to be reduced to four times a year and phased out before Paul was permanently placed. Mary went along with this plan, but when suitable adopters were recently identified for Paul, his mother was only prepared to agree if her contact continued.

The local authority had not sought coercive powers but the child's mother was never given clear information about her rights as the only person with parental responsibility. Contact arrangements were made while the mother was still in shock and later she was afraid to jeopardise her son's future by being unco-operative. Only when faced with imminent and final separation, did she pluck up courage to speak out. Local authorities should never be prescriptive about contact with children who are accommodated and should be open to families' changing needs and capacities.

When children are accommodated, contact arrangements may be flexible and supervision will rarely be necessary to protect them. Parents must be seen as capable of co-operation and of having their children returned to them. *Contact: Managing visits to children looked after away from home,*[6] published by BAAF, is a useful book for social workers trying to make the most of contact.

Contact when children are in care

Contact arrangements for children who are "in care" are subject to the directions of the court. A balance has to be struck between maintaining contact for a child and ensuring that the child is not placed at risk of further harm. By definition, a child is "in care" or care is sought, because they are believed to be at risk of significant harm, and therefore the factors which have led to care proceedings will inevitably have an impact upon contact arrangements.

The greatest attention should be paid to negotiation between the parties in advance of court hearings. The role of the guardian *ad litem* at this stage is central in focusing the attention of all concerned upon the best interests of the child. Other social workers in care proceedings can easily feel that they are held in low esteem. Their practice and planning may be held up to rigorous scrutiny from child care "experts" and legal representatives alike. Furthermore, the care proceedings may be impeding their work with families. Much has been made recently about the challenge of working in partnership in child protection, but there is an equal, if not greater, challenge in working in partnership when children are "in care". For once a care order is granted, the involvement of the guardian *ad litem* and the court is at an end, and social workers are left to pick up the pieces. It is not without some cause that local authorities are suspected of making commitments in court, which they are unable to maintain in practice, especially as the making of a care order could be the point at which contact arrangements are reduced.

Case
>   After supervising contact to four children over the previous nine months and providing excellent observations for the court, a sessional worker was taken off the case when care orders were made. Contact was to be significantly reduced, but the loss of the supervisor placed all subsequent plans in jeopardy.

Parents may have great difficulty in accepting decisions concerning contact with their children in care. They are more likely to be able to work with the decisions handed down in court, if there is effective partnership, so that they are informed of developments; if there is openness and honesty, their feelings of loss, anger and failure will not be dismissed.

When a child is "in care" the duty imposed upon a local authority to promote contact is secondary to the safety of the child. In extreme cases, if safety cannot be assured, specific contact can be terminated.

Plans, agreements and contracts
A "contact plan" is essential for all children who are looked after by local authorities, whether they are "in care" or "accommodated". Care plans

in which contact arrangements are addressed, are obligatory for children "in care". In marked contrast one could have difficulty in locating a contact plan for a child who is accommodated. Plans should be written down; they should represent collective opinion and be drawn up as an agreement or even in more formal terms, as a contract. The language of the plan must be plain; expectations should be clear; the plan should be reviewable, and indicate what will happen if it needs to be amended or is challenged.

It is worth noting that several formats for contact plans are being developed. While these printed forms can neatly fit local authority requirements, there is a danger that they will standardise arrangements rather than encourage creativity to meet individual needs.

When making a plan for contact, we should specify the form contact will take, with whom it will be, where it will take place, when and how often; if contact is to be supervised, what is the purpose and how will it be done. Awareness of race, culture, class and religion must be demonstrated; plans must represent a commitment to, and belief in, equality of opportunities, and not pay mere lip service to the idea.

What form of contact?
Face-to-face, direct contact
This is the most normal way for children and parents to meet. In exceptional circumstances, direct contact may be conditional on acceptable behaviour and it may have to be supervised. Some children find videos a welcome substitute if there are reasons why they should not meet with their parents.

Letters, cards and presents
Children and families often need support to read and write letters and cards, which can become treasured possessions, tangible proof of connections, as well as celebrations of anniversaries. In another sense indirect contact can be used to place a safe distance between children and their families.

Case
Joanne who is eight, and Lloyd who is ten have been "in care" since

1992 as a result of serious harm. Their parents continue to have severe mental health problems and there is no prospect of rehabilitation. The children are settled together in a long-term foster placement. Neither wishes to see their parents of whom they have only painful memories. The children have asked to be protected from them. Under the care plan, contact has been restricted to Christmas and birthday cards from the parents. This has reassured the children by setting absolute limits on contact, while the parents are relieved that a degree of contact is being maintained.

Telephone contact

Very properly, children in residential care are increasingly given a phonecard and access to a private phone; however, the telephone is not an easy way to keep in touch. Unexpected or unsolicited telephone calls can compound existing difficulties. When telephone contact is agreed, foster carers, social workers and residential workers should be aware that telephone calls, like visits, have to be given attention.

Case

After a succession of disruptions, Craig was eventually placed in secure accommodation. Contact with his family was by then non-existent. Previous phone calls had been rare and fraught. The social worker and secure unit staff co-operated to prepare both Craig and his family to make and receive phone calls. For Craig, this meant role play and planning conversations, which previously had lapsed into abuse before abruptly coming to an end. The family had to be encouraged to persevere and not to be put off by initial rejections. Regular telephone contact was eventually established.

If telephone contact is too threatening, or not practicable, cassettes, which can be more easily controlled, may prove an alternative.

Photographs

Photographs are treasures to keep and gifts to send for any child living away from home. A camera is one of the most essential tools available to social workers, in order to photograph not only children but also their families.

Information

School reports, medical reports, certificates or achievement awards, should be shared with parents in almost all circumstances if children are in care. If they are accommodated, information concerning the children should be given to the parents automatically.

"Letterbox service"

Indirect contact is often maintained via social services or other agencies. It should be more than just a facility for redirecting mail. An effective letterbox service should be personalised with a named worker to support and monitor the exchange of news.

With whom?

Parents and step-parents

While contact may serve a crucial role in maintaining existing relationships, arrangements should accommodate developments, such as a parent taking a new partner. Where parents are in dispute with one another, social workers would be well advised to develop mediation skills or to use mediation services, to establish agreement and limit needless conflict.

Siblings, half siblings and step-siblings

It is one of the principles of the Children Act that siblings should be placed together whenever possible, or at least to remain in regular contact. In practice, compromises have to be made as we struggle to balance the best interests of individual children against those of the sibling group. It has to be accepted that resources are not always available to keep siblings together, and it is therefore all the more important that local authorities have clear policies to support contact between siblings who have to be separated.

Case

Half sisters Jade who is nine, Caroline thirteen, and Lucy fourteen, were accommodated following their mother's suicide. No other family members were able to provide accommodation for all three children for whom a residential placement was located, albeit 60 miles from their home area. The sisters gained strength from being placed together at the beginning, but when they were placed with foster carers in their home area six months later, their conflicting needs became more apparent. The children were separated but regular contact was built into their placement plans. Two of the girls were placed sufficiently close to one another to share in recreational activities such as swimming and majorettes. Two way contact was made with Jade, whose needs were best met in a specialist residential placement.

Whereas pre-adolescent siblings tend to be looked after as a group, and become known as "the Johnson girls" or "the Jones children", older children who need to be looked after are usually away from home on their own. All sibling relationships should be nurtured, not forgetting contact with adult brothers and sisters already living independently, and with siblings born while children are being looked after by a local authority. Our connections with siblings are the longest in our lives, and we must not risk that children who are already losing much, should lose more.

Grandparents and step-grandparents
Grandparents represent the continuity of generations. Even if they were not successful parents themselves, they can be affectionate grandparents with the necessary time to spare for their grandchildren. They may also prove to be key figures at the centre of the extended family or cultural network. As social workers, we are sometimes too quick to overlook the value of grandparents unless they can provide a child with a bed. It is our responsibility to find a child somewhere to sleep; grandparents can go on being grandparents, even if they do not have a spare room.

Extended family, friends and neighbours
Most of us have aunts, uncles and cousins we would not care to lose and we should not allow children in our care to do so, nor should the notion of family be restricted to blood ties. Cultural differences regarding extended families must not be misunderstood due to ignorance or

prejudice. If we listen to the wishes and feelings of children, we will hear who is important to them. They may want to keep in touch with a neighbour, a school friend, a teacher, a foster family or a previous social worker; all these people, and more, may hold their past together.

Where?

The setting has to be appropriate to the purpose and promotion of contact, but must also ensure the child's safety. Creative and imaginative social work can make contact meaningful in the most unlikely settings, but this is no cause for complacency. If local authorities are to value contact in practice, then a range of venues should be available.

Home

If a child's safety is not at stake, there can be contact in the family home, which may include overnight stays, when contact is part of a rehabilitation plan. Home contact should be monitored but not treated as a reward or a privilege.

Children often have to be accommodated to give the various parties a break; home contact with social work support can provide an opportunity for relationships to be tested and renegotiated, although hostilities can resurface and place further contact at risk.

Hospital or prison

Children are frequently accommodated if their main carer is hospitalised or imprisoned. While contact is desirable, visits can be harrowing for all concerned. Children should be prepared for adults being heavily medicated, wired up to a battery of medical technology, or under surveillance. Planning and liaison with other agencies is required to avoid undue or needless distress to children and parents alike.

Foster homes

Foster carers can play a major part in contact arrangements, in many cases providing both a venue and supervision. However, foster carers' homes should be used only by choice, and not as a substitute for more costly alternatives. The resourcefulness, warmth and patience of many foster carers who offer their home for contact is remarkable, but can feel threatening to parents who cannot cope equally well.

Contact centres and family centres

Social workers should be aware of local contact centres which exist to assist children of separated and divorced parents. Contact centres can provide a discreet, child-centred, neutral setting, which is sensitive towards adults and carers for "normal" activities, like sharing a meal and playing together. Family centres can be excellent for supervised contact, to say nothing of the fact that costs can be borne "in house". Staff in local authority family centres are increasingly able to supervise contact as part of an observation and assessment programme. Social services day nurseries, children's centres and residential units can sometimes provide a room for contact, with supervision if necessary.

Case

The Charles family, from which three children have been taken into care, has had past dealings with a day nursery. Staff at the nursery had a positive relationship with Mr and Mrs Charles and regular contact has been established at the nursery, once a month, for the whole family. The setting is familiar and parents as well as children trust the nursery staff who supervise the contact.

The use of family support services, as in this example, should reflect an organisational commitment to contact, rather than be dependent upon goodwill on the part of workers.

Other venues

Resourceful social work can promote contact in libraries, shopping centres, a park with a playground, a zoo, a burger bar, or anywhere ordinary parents take ordinary children. One place which should only be used in an emergency is the local authority social services office; it will not do to make a conference room or interview room double as a contact venue.

Practical considerations of venue

The Children Act and accompanying guidance direct that if children are to be placed away from home, they should be placed within a reasonable distance: 'walkable or within a half-hour journey by public transport.' Travel costs can be paid and so can telephone calls. If distance is unavoidable, many residential units are now able to provide visitors with overnight accommodation.

Social workers should avoid the assumption that if parents are sufficiently motivated they will make their own transport arrangements. We must take the lead in such matters. The provision of taxis or escorts may prove a more reliable alternative to public transport, especially if a continuity of drivers or escorts can be arranged. If families have their own transport, a contribution by the local authority towards petrol or even the upkeep of the vehicle, may be a relatively cheap option.

When?

The timing of contact should not be dictated by limited resources. "Out of hours" contact may prove difficult for social workers, but there is no reason why children should be ruled by "office hours". Contact may need to be arranged after school, at weekends, on birthdays, public holidays, to mark different religious festivals and on other special occasions. This might seem obvious, but it is not always remembered.

Case

Fifteen-year-old Attiqur was looked after in a residential setting, following a breakdown in relationships at home. Shortly after he was accommodated, Ramadan commenced. Given the delicate family situation, contact was promoted between Attiqur and community leaders at Attiqur's request. As well as residential staff respecting Attiqur's need to fast, it was essential that he observe religious celebrations and attend prayers at the mosque. Support for Attiqur to maintain his contacts and religious observances led in part to his return home.

How often?

It is remarkable how much contact can be arranged with adequate resources and commitment. Nevertheless, quantity should not be at the expense of quality. Parents will frequently press for more, when they really want it to be better. Perhaps an adage should be established along the lines of 'Look after the quality of contact and the quantity will look after itself'. How often will then depend on the age of the child, the circumstances and the aims of contact.

Case

Thomas, who is in a long-term foster placement, saw his mother four times a year as stipulated in a S.34 order. After his mother had repeatedly applied for increased contact without success, Thomas was heard by the guardian *ad litem* to say that he did not want more contact: 'I just want it to be all right when I see her.' Previous contact had been disastrous, with each blaming the other for past failures. After their last meeting, Thomas had threatened 'Next time I'm going to knife her,' while his mother said, 'I'm not going to put up with this, next time I'll hit him'. Contact had been grudgingly set up to adhere to the letter of the law only. Thomas's social worker did not appreciate the spirit of the court's ruling. With preparation and positive planning, the next session was an enjoyable occasion and this quality has been maintained. Significantly, Thomas's mother has made no further application for increased contact.

Supervision

The implications of supervised contact have received scant attention, yet for social workers and their managers "supervised contact" can prove a massive, time-consuming and frequently stressful task. "Supervised contact" requires the local authority to promote contact while taking steps to protect the child. All cases of supervised contact are complex, some are merely more complex than others.

Supervision is a planned response to concerns that a child may be at risk during direct contact. Supervision may take the form of discreet observation at a distance, or involve active participation by the supervisor to encourage interactions, or to ensure a child's safety, if a parent is suspected of having Munchausen by Proxy Syndrome or if there has been sexual abuse.

The reason for supervision should be stated in a contact plan, together with specific conditions, for example, that parents must not be under the influence of alcohol or non-prescriptive drugs. Expectations of parental co-operation and agreed reasonable behaviour can also be written in, but we have to beware of imposing our own views of what is reasonable. Given that supervised contact will be stressful under even the most ideal circumstances, the supervisor's task should include planning and debriefing with parents and the child, if old enough, before and after each visit. Several questions arise: What will they say or do, what will they bring with them, what do they expect might happen, and how will they cope with conflict? And afterwards – how does it feel now, what succeeded and what can be better next time. Skilled supervisors also need skilled supervision.

Case

The four children of the Kay family had been repeatedly neglected by their mother over the past four years. Their father had deserted the family some six years ago. After several periods of accommodation and evidence of physical abuse, an application for care proceedings was made and contact carefully planned. Extensive work with the family revealed the conflicting interests of the children and it was agreed they should not be placed together in care.

Two experienced social workers were allocated and a sessional worker was engaged to supervise contact. In one week contact could be: mother and eldest daughter, mother and three youngest children, mother and all four children, or a meeting of just the four siblings. The sessional worker managed all transport arrangements and liaised with the family centre venue, foster carers, schools and both social workers. The social workers prepared Mrs Kay and the children for contact, by role playing visits and practising conversation; afterwards they discussed with them how it went and how they felt about it. Contact sessions were often stressful and linking one session to the next was crucial. The children and their mother developed close relationships with the supervisor. She was able to support Mrs Kay and to represent the children at the many meetings and reviews.

Regular supported contact was maintained over almost ten months and even though it effectively demonstrated that rehabilitation would not be possible, the mother was able to accept her own limitations and to observe the extreme needs of her children. Care orders were subsequently made and, with a view to long-term placements, reduced levels of contact have been agreed. The sessional worker, regarded as a help by the mother and as a protector by the children, will continue to supervise the contact.

It is natural for children to have contact with their families, but the arrangements of supervised contact inevitably give rise to a degree of artificiality. If the contact setting is experienced as too unreal, parents will feel unable to behave normally, or else they will opt out of the contact altogether. Either way, they will be blamed for not responding to their children. When supervised contact is part of a plan for observation and assessment, social workers must be aware of the pressure this places on parents, especially for those who believe that their contact is being supervised purely so that the local authority can gather evidence against them. For many parents being observed is "like being in a goldfish bowl".

Finally, the question of who supervises contact needs careful consideration. Most social workers do not have the time required for effective supervision. Local authorities would do well to train and build up a pool of experienced sessional workers as contact supervisors and co-ordinators. Alternatively, the service could be contracted out to voluntary organisations. Experienced supervisors would develop skills in assessing the quality of contact and attachment, information which is vital in reaching decisions when applications for care are made or when termination of contact is under consideration.

If foster carers are asked to supervise contact, it should be recognised that they could be placed in a compromising situation, especially if contact takes place away from the foster carer's home. Foster carers who do supervise contact should be appropriately rewarded. We should never assume that supervision of contact by foster carers comes in a package marked "foster care".

Contact orders and termination of contact

It is still early days for a detailed assessment of how S.34 contact orders under the 1989 Children Act are being used. The recent study by the Social Services Inspectorate of four local authorities[7] noted that in some cases there are specific orders regarding contact arrangements, whereas in other similar cases there are no such orders. Contact arrangements which are part of the care plan are taken into consideration before a care order is made, but they are not legally binding. Specific orders under S.34(5) *are* legally binding.

S.34 also contains provision for termination of contact. Under subsection 4 'the court may make an order authorising the local authority to refuse to allow contact' between the child and anyone with whom contact could otherwise be promoted.

Despite the now widely accepted belief that contact should be promoted, there are extreme situations where it is in a child's best interest that contact with a particular person should be terminated. This decision is not one which a court takes lightly; however, anecdotal evidence suggests that social workers are over cautious and turn too readily to doomed alternatives. On the other hand, the SSI study observes that a number of social workers 'thought that the courts were inclined to go beyond "the extra mile" to give parents every opportunity to prove their worth'. Courts and wavering social workers can give parents false hopes, and when the decision to terminate contact is eventually made, it becomes an even more painful situation with little scope for working together.

Under the 1989 Children Act, children who are accommodated may be a party to a S.8 contact order. While the aim should always be to work through voluntary agreements, it is possible that accommodated children will need a S.8 contact order to specify contact with a particular person, for example, a father who has not been included in arrangements which have led to his child being accommodated. S.8 contact orders can be used by accommodated children who are separated from their siblings and need to take steps to ensure they have contact. A local authority cannot be a party to a S.8 order but it does have a duty to support and promote contact arrangements, which may include a S.8 contact order.

Conclusion

Local authorities do recognise the importance of maintaining contact when children are looked after, and on the whole, practice reflects creditably on social workers and the agencies involved. With a commitment to working in partnership, and a belief in contact as a child's right, local authorities are making good contact plans, and sometimes they are making contact arrangements which are a triumph in the face of adversity.

At a time when social work with children and families is dominated by child protection, family contact for children who are looked after could easily be undervalued. Care plans define the contact arrangements for those children who are subject to care orders, but the majority of children who are looked after are accommodated. Agreements which describe the form contact will take should be standard practice for all children looked after by a local authority.

The welfare of the child is paramount and any risk to a child during contact must be avoided. The supervision of contact is a complex, demanding and frequently exhausting task, which requires skill on the part of workers and investment of time and money on the part of local authorities.

For most children who are looked after by local authorities, "contact" is not problematic, but contact must also be purposeful. It must be planned and adequately resourced. There has been no further guidance on contact since the Code of Practice on Access to Children in Care issued in 1983; this should now be remedied with a review of contact issues for all children who are looked after. The Children Act represents a transformation of thinking by turning access into contact. Effective partnerships between local authorities, families, social workers, and support agencies point to a way ahead. As social workers, we must not forget that our most important partnership is with the child who is looked after, and that all children have a right to stay connected to their families of origin.

References

1. Millham S, Bullock R, Hosie K, and Little M, *Access Disputes in Child Care*, Gower, 1989.

2. Department of Health, *The Challenge of Partnership in Child Protection: Practice guide*, HMSO,1995.

3. Gibson P, and Parsloe P, 'What stops parental access to children in care', *Adoption & Fostering*, 8:1, BAAF, 1984.

4. Berridge D, and Cleaver H, *Foster Home Breakdown*, Blackwell, 1987.

5. Marsh P, 'Changing Practice in Child Care – The Children Act 1989', *Adoption & Fostering* 14:4, BAAF, 1990.

6. Hess P M, and Proch K O, *Contact: Managing visits to children looked after away from home*, BAAF, 1993.

7. Social Services Inspectorate/Department of Health, *Contact Orders Study: Experiences in local authorities of public law applications involving issues of contact for children with their parents and families*, SSI, 1994.

5 The significance and meaning of contact for black families
A practitioner's view

Rose Dagoo

Rose Dagoo is an adoption specialist, a Guardian ad litem, and a Social Work Consultant.

In this paper, the term "black" refers to people of African or Asian origins and contact includes face to face, telephone and postal contact.

Following the implementation of the Children Act 1989, increasing attention is being given to contact arrangements for children looked after in local authority care. There is an expectation coming from the courts that this matter will be addressed by all the parties involved, including unmarried fathers, the extended family, solicitors, guardians *ad litem*, social workers and other interested parties. This focus on contact has generated much debate and many articles and books on the subject. However, scanning the literature on issues of contact concerning black families, there is a noticeable death of material. This leads to uninformed practice and a corresponding reduction in the quality of service offered to black families and children. All too often we tend to rely on studies of African American families for our reference points. But this ignores the vast difference in patterns of family life and the historical context in which these patterns have developed.

In this chapter I would like to concentrate on two main issues relating to contact and illustrate them with case examples:
- The principle of partnership (1989 Children Act), as perceived by black families and their extended kin in establishing and maintaining contact.
- Factors which serve to undermine contact between black families and their children.

Separation from those we love and from our nearest and dearest is always a painful and distressing experience. This is true irrespective of race, culture and religion. A priority for professionals working with children in the care system and with those family members they cherish, is to find ways of reducing the pangs of separation.

Like white parents, black parents feel a deep sense of guilt and failure when their children are removed from their care. All too often, because they are unable to put it into words, these feelings find expression in their behaviour towards the people close to them and those in authority. Additionally, black parents are intimidated and at times overwhelmed by the intervention of the state whose officials in authority are, in the main, white. Even in situations where direct work is done by black professionals, parents believe that the decision makers and those with ultimate authority are white. For black families, life in a predominantly white society and their personal encounters with authority create an undercurrent of fear, distrust and insecurity which filter into relationships with professionals who are involved with their children. Black families have an expectation that discrimination will usually be part of any bureaucratic process, however unintentional it might be. This can lead them to react defensively, to seem angry and unco-operative. Parents can then become difficult to engage with and may appear threatening to some professionals.

Engaging with parents and other members of the extended family is crucial for contact arrangements. This requires patience, experience and tact; seemingly small things can tip the balance against it. For instance, older people expect to be referred to by their surnames and addressed formally with the prefix Miss, Mrs or Mr. To be called by their first names by someone younger, irrespective of status, is regarded as over familiar and utterly disrespectful. A worker's behaviour in a family's home signals the respect the family will be shown. Regard for religious rituals, such as taking off shoes before entering the living area, or asking if unsure of the custom, will set the tone. If anxious workers, eager to please, go into the kitchen to make coffee, it is not necessarily seen as helpful but as an arrogant disregard of privacy and boundaries.

Parents whose self-esteem and confidence have been eroded by years of deprivation and discrimination have developed sensitivities which can very easily be bruised. Their tolerance of thoughtless and inconsiderate professional practice is limited. An example often cited by parents is the disregard for a family's routine: appointments are made at short notice, without allowance for other demands on the family's time, and cancelled at the last minute, with apologies and explanations not readily forthcoming.

The black extended family generally plays a meaningful part in family affairs. When assessments have to be made or life story material collected for children, the extended kin could provide a mine of information. It is essential to probe for details about these relatives, some of whom may not really be related but are longstanding friends of the family. If they are reluctant to come forward, this should not be interpreted as a lack of concern or not wanting to be involved. It is more likely to be inhibition rooted in distrust of white authority, lack of confidence in dealing with social institutions, and uncertainty about the workings of the welfare state and the relevant legislation.

Absent fathers
It is not uncommon for workers to overlook the significance of absent unmarried fathers, grandparents and other relatives who seem to have become estranged from the family, but may have retained links unbeknown to the professionals. It is usually assumed that black, absent, unmarried fathers are not interested in their children's welfare. While this is true of some, it should not be an assumption made about all of them. Their detachment could be the product of years of exclusion from decision making and negative confrontations with officialdom. Anecdotal evidence suggests that a large section of black males have been unjustly stopped and harassed by the police; social services can easily be perceived as another form of social policing.

Culture clashes
Lack of knowledge of the different cultures of black children has undermined the forging and nurturing of contact, even when such contact was deemed to be in the children's best interests.

Case
    Lorna, a young woman who spent a large part of her childhood and

adolescence in a children's home, found her mother after years of searching for her. When the children's home closed and the care staff moved away, she had no caring adult or relative to whom she could have turned in adversity. She recalled that her mother, 'an old black woman dressed rather oddly,' used to visit her at the home. The other children would laugh at her, and Lorna remembers denying that the woman was her mother, out of utter embarrassment. On the only two occasions Lorna went home to see her mother, she complained that she was forced to drink a foul tasting cough syrup for a cold. When asked by residential staff if she wanted to continue with home visits, she said 'no', remembering the cough syrup. She still remembers that no-one took the time to find out how she was feeling about a mother from whom she had been separated since infancy, or to explain this mother's 'strangeness'. Raised in a predominantly white children's home by white staff, Lorna had very little understanding of her mother's race and culture, and therefore of her own. Being made to drink a foul tasting cough syrup was a customary homespun remedy for colds and influenza in many Caribbean households at the time. While Lorna passed through the care system before the 1989 Children Act, similar stories continue to emerge.

Ignorance of a family's culture can lead to misinterpretations which may then have the effect of restricting vital contact.

Case

Samuel, a West African baby, was removed from his home on an emergency protection order. The child was found to have unexplained fractures and was hospitalised together with his mother, while investigations were made. When Samuel was removed from his mother, who was on her own in England at the time, she cried inconsolably while rocking and dancing and clinging to her child. The medical and social work staff, believing her behaviour to be indicative of a mental breakdown, called the police to take her to the local psychiatric hospital. Several police officers arrived and she was arrested, handcuffed and taken to a psychiatric hospital. The psychiatrist, recognising the mother's intense distress at the enforced separation from her son, discharged her. In West Africa, grief and mourning are expressed through rocking and dancing.

Black people, and black women in particular, are sometimes diagnosed as mentally ill, when their depression stems from their socio-economic circumstances and not from any kind of psychiatric disturbance. If they cannot look after their children because they are depressed, and the local authority has to look after them, then the label of mental illness will affect the contact arrangements.

The following situation further illustrates the cultural dimension.

Case

Ten-year-old Kerri had lived with her maternal grandmother since the age of five. She was made the subject of a care order after her young mother became overwhelmed by the responsibility of caring for a child. At first Kerri was fostered, but then her grandmother was able to give up her job to look after her. Sadly, Kerri eventually proved too much for her grandmother because she could not manage Kerri's unruly and aggressive behaviour. The years of neglect and ill treatment when Kerri had lived with her mother had left her an angry, distrustful and unhappy child. In the classroom she disrupted the other pupils and was exhausting for teachers. She was finally excluded permanently from school.

Kerri was taken away from her grandmother and placed in a children's home some distance away. Her grandmother was reluctant to let Kerri go, denying that there were any problems. She was content to keep Kerri at home with a few hours tuition a week although she knew Kerri was a particularly able child, assessed at above average but not working to her potential. Her grandmother was allowed to visit Kerri every week at the children's home and was given assistance with travel expenses, but Kerri was not allowed to visit her.

This severing of connection with her home and neighbourhood, where she had lived since the age of five and regularly visited since she was born, was thought to be in Kerri's best interests. Explanations as to how social workers had arrived at this decision were not given to the grandmother, which served to alienate her and did little to gain her co-operation with their care plans. Her requests for Kerri to have home visits met with dismissal. As a consequence, the grandmother became more critical of the care Kerri received in the children's home and this, in turn, became an irritant to the care staff. Her visits were only tolerated, and the goodies she brought her grand-daughter became an excuse for the staff's disapproval of her.

Each week, Kerri's grandmother would bring home-cooked food which she knew was Kerri's favourite. In Caribbean and Asian cultures food is a focal point around which socialising takes place. It is a way of demonstrating care, and much time and effort is put into its preparation. The home regarded these treats as unnecessary and overlooked the continuity it provided for Kerri, who had been wrenched away from everything that was familiar and comforting to her.

In this atmosphere of attrition, the grandmother's devotion to Kerri and the unfailing love and concern she showed during the weekly contact, were disregarded. Yet her grandmother demonstrated in a concrete way to Kerri that she was loved and wanted; for a child as isolated as Kerri was, this at least helped to protect her self-esteem.

Social services had stopped contact between Kerri and her mother five years earlier, because Kerri had suffered physical harm. However, over the years Kerri's mother had begun to lead a more settled life and was reconciled with her own mother (Kerri's grandmother), who had let her visit Kerri occasionally. The family was nervous about sharing this with the authorities, fearing that it would be misconstrued and prohibited. It did not come to light until Kerri's placement in the children's home, that her mother had resumed informal contact. Kerri had been talking to the care staff about her mother and they became convinced that Kerri should see her.

Kerri's father had been discouraged from having contact by her mother and grandmother after they fell out with him. But from time to time he would meet Kerri in the street while she lived with her grandmother and he would make a point of acknowledging her. He was never seen by Kerri's social worker to ascertain his wishes about contact, although he had made tentative efforts to communicate his interests to the department. He had been living in the neighbourhood for years and was quite accessible.

Kerri was allocated a new social worker, and what could have been an opportunity to re-evaluate past decisions about contact in view of changes in the family, was missed and these decisions were taken as set in stone and fixed for all time. This approach did not take into account that families can change and that contact arrangements need to be flexible to respond to such changes.

Kerri's interest in her father was stifled by her mother and grandmother who had become embittered about him. Social services compounded the damage by stereotyping him as a negligent black father. But some direct work with Kerri would have revealed her longing to get to know him. Her mother's contact with her need not have been furtive. Contact with her grandmother could have been better facilitated, and the requests for home visits merited unbiased consideration. Kerri would have been ready to open up about the important people in her life, had her social worker been receptive and not been bogged down by her family's past history.

In the end it was the grandmother's intervention through the court which brought cultural clashes about contact to the forefront. The local authority was directed to take a fresh look at their past decisions and contact plans. The judge who heard the application commented that had the proper work been done, this matter need never have come to court.

Kerri's case reveals how the principle of partnership is experienced by black families. Practitioners must be conscious of the particular considerations necessary to engage black families so that negotiations around contact can take place. When planning contact for children who are looked after by the local authority, social workers must be aware of the impact on black families, and the consequences of living in a society where authority rests with the ethnic majority.

Further reading

Hill R B, *Informal Adoption among Black Families*, National Urban League Research Department, 1977.

Banks N, 'Children of black mixed parentage and their placement needs', *Adoption & Fostering*, 19:2, BAAF, 1995.

Research which has a bearing on adoption or on alternatives to adoption, DOH Social Services Inspectorate,1993.

'Transcultural Psychiatry: Racism and mental illness', *International Journal of Psychiatry*, Spring 1984.

6   Do children have a right to leave their pasts behind them?
Contact with children who have been abused

Gerrilyn Smith

Gerrilyn Smith is a Clinical Psychologist, Family Therapist, trainer and consultant with expertise on issues of abuse in families.

In this chapter I discuss contact, or rather the objections to contact, if children have been abused by their families of origin. The general child care policy of encouraging contact is fully supported, but there is a need to consider those circumstances in which continued contact is not in the child's interest. Comments made to me by professionals and foster carers indicate the need for clearer guidance about whether and when all contact, both direct and indirect, should be suspended for a period of time.

Sexual abuse necessarily involves emotional and physical abuse. Consequently, in thinking about abuse of children, I see it as a progressive failure to meet children's needs escalating to perverted and distorted relationships based on sexual gratification, exploitation and coercive control.

Consideration has to be given to the child's ability to articulate wishes and feelings regarding ongoing contact, and more attention should be paid to behavioural indicators of stress. In a recent article entitled "Linking research evidence and practice in fostering work",[1] the authors note four key factors linked to outcome in placements. Behavioural problems prior to placement are identified as predictive of negative outcomes in placement. However, it is unclear if ongoing behavioural problems that were present prior to placement are positively correlated with contact. Children can find it very difficult to settle or feel protected if they are still in contact with people who have abused them in the past.

For example, at a recent training event on life story work, one foster mother told how the four-year-old child she was fostering would cry and scream every time she took her to have contact with her parents. The contact sessions necessitated a car journey, and the little girl would have to be strapped into her car seat by the foster mother who also drove the child to the session. The child was inconsolable. It was known she had been physically and sexually abused by her parents but the plan was to return her home to their care, hence a very rigorous contact programme had been planned. In the end, the foster carer refused to take the child to the sessions, as she felt it compromised her position as protector to the child. How did the child experience the enforced taking to contact sessions by her current primary caregiver? How did she then experience the foster mother no longer attending?

This kind of story is not unusual, and the feedback the child is giving regarding her experience appears to be ignored by the professionals involved in her care with the exception of her primary caregiver, who feels she has to withdraw. To the experienced foster mother, it was clear that this child was not able to cope with contact and needed, at the very least, a break. This was raised with the professional network but both the child's feedback and the foster carer's comments on the impact of contact were disregarded. There is clearly a necessity for more detailed guidance, support and supervision regarding contact issues both for the professionals and the primary caregivers, who often have to implement contact arrangements devised by others, which they may be fundamentally opposed to.

This scenario suggests to me that the need to re-examine contact in the light of traumatic experiences within families of origin is absolutely essential. It is also important to note that the current "back to basics" campaign, which emphasises nuclear families and their importance, coincides with the present backlash against recognising the extent of family violence in all its forms. The Children Act[2] could consequently be used as a reactionary vehicle to maintain families at all costs and to place parent's needs (and right) for contact, above the best interest of the child.

What contact can contribute
Contact is a clinical term that describes an experience of meeting with

significant members of one's family. Traditionally, this operates on a continuum from open and unrestricted contact to theoretically no contact at all. Within this continuum is the category of indirect contact which includes phone calls, letters and photos. But the word contact also implies a connectedness or meaningful interaction and is frequently viewed as having positive value only.

June Thoburn has written that contact supports the child's sense of continuity and identity.[3] However, we need to remind ourselves that sometimes the state intervenes into family life expressly in order to disrupt continuity and to provide children with alternative family experiences; not necessarily to replace or substitute their family of origin but to broaden the child's repertoire of relational skills and to offer corrective messages or, as Vera Fahlberg would say, a re-parenting experience.[4] Identity work can be done without face to face contact. Indirect contact through letters, phone calls, and photos can contribute material from parents and extended family which may need to be held in trust until a time appropriate for the child.

Continuity depends on the child having established an attachment. In my clinical practice, I have seen children whose sense of attachment to their family of origin appears, on assessment, to be non-existent. As a consequence, there is little to build on through continued contact with parents. Additionally, contact with the wider community needs to be considered, especially for children from minority ethnic families. Black family placements for black children are an essential part of helping a black child establish a positive identity. Contact with religious institutions, educational establishments, language classes, for example, can help to establish a child within an historical and political context. This too forms part of one's identity and reminds us all that skin colour is but one aspect of our identity.

Disconnection from their community is an issue for many families where abuse occurs, so it can be especially important to promote contacts with the extended family and the wider community. Sometimes these contacts are more important than those with the nuclear family.

There has to be a flexibility in contact arrangements that allows for them to be regularly reviewed and varied if necessary. For many children who have been abused and placed away from their parents when very young, a suspension of contact may be necessary to begin their recovery work. But during adolescence they may wish to explore their family of origin more directly. These changing needs should be accommodated. Plans and preparation work for all involved need to be made which include the need for supervision and an assessment of the level of risk such renewed contact may pose for the child.

Exceptional circumstances

The question of direct or indirect contact has to be re-examined in the light of our increasing knowledge regarding the impact of trauma on a child's development. Much of what is written about contact fails to address this issue. For example, in a recent summary of research into contact and permanent placement by Ryburn,[5] there is only one mention of abuse. This referred to a North American study of 719 adoptions;[6] some (number unspecified) involved children with a history of maltreatment. As someone who works in the field of child protection, when reading material on contact I feel peculiarly distanced from what I read.

In cases of sexual abuse, contact may impede the child's recovery by keeping the traumatic material alive. This needs to be said clearly and unequivocally. Instead, I read that the only contra-indication for continuing contact is open hostility and conflict,[7] while another study quoted indicates that the benefits, even in situations of open hostility, may outweigh the disadvantages.[8] This review of the literature is coupled with a terse dismissal of the clinical experience of Anna Freud and colleagues, whose conclusions on contact were considered not to have had an empirical basis. Reading this, I begin to feel as the foster mother did – a lone voice whimpering in a sea of empirical evidence which contradicts my clinical experience.

Professionals should explore the meaning of contact for children, and accept that we as outsiders to the family process, may not understand certain interactions in the contact sessions. In a recent study on incest and its meaning,[9] Patricia Phelan found that most fathers initiated sexual activity by using non-verbal means to extend and pervert normal family routines and interactions. Thus non-verbal messages even in supervised contact sessions will serve to reinforce the power and authority of the abuser as well as activate old abusive family patterns. As a consequence, contact may hinder the child's recovery and ability to make use of safe placements. Some clinical examples may be useful in illustrating these points.

Contact with an abuser

Case

Laura was a four-year-old white girl referred for assessment following concerns regarding sexual abuse. There were medical signs of inter-ference. She had a high level of behavioural disturbance including bedwetting, headbanging, nightmares and self harming (biting herself). She had disclosed to her mother and other extended members of her family that her daddy had hurt her, giving explicit detail of the sexual nature of her hurt.

Among the issues for consideration was whether she should have contact with her father following confirmation of the allegation of sexual abuse and the separation of her parents. The mother recorded the child's behaviour in a diary including the frequency of wet beds, episodes of self harm and night terrors, while Laura was having twice weekly supervised contact with her father pending matrimonial court proceedings. The level of behavioural disturbance was extremely high, with episodes in every category recorded on a daily basis and continuous wet beds. As part of the assessment procedure, contact was suspended for a period of time. During the time of no contact, the behavioural disturbance gradually diminished including a return to dry beds at night. Toward the end of the assessment period, which spanned 16 weeks, another supervised contact was arranged between Laura and her father.

Laura was delighted to see her father and played games with him. On several occasions she asked if he was alright and if he was going to hurt her. This was the only sign of anxiety manifested in the contact session itself. Following the session, her distressing behaviour returned. On the train journey home she was biting herself. That night she wet the bed after a terrible nightmare when she called out to her mother that the monster was going to get her. She was defiant and rude to her mother. This behaviour peaked very soon after the contact, rapidly escalating from no recorded episodes to many, then gradually diminishing over two weeks.

The change in Laura's behaviour was also noted by her nursery school. There was evidence that the behavioural disturbance seriously impeded her capacity to learn and to manage her peer relationships when she was uncharacteristically involved in an aggressive outburst with another child. It seemed clear that contact with her father was profoundly disturbing for her. The recommendation was that contact should be suspended, until she was of an age to protect herself. Indirect contact in the form of letters and cards was managed and supervised by Laura's mother. She regularly writes the required newsletter, enclosing school photos and pictures Laura wishes to send. All cards and letters received, she keeps to give to her daughter when she is older. No requests have been made by Laura to see her father. She understands that he is not seeing her because he hurt her. There are no behavioural disturbances and she is doing well in school and other aspects of her development.

Case

Amelia, a ten-year-old white girl, was sexually abused by her mother. This was disclosed when Amelia was eight. During assessment, when Amelia was asked to draw a picture of her family, she drew the family cats. The quality of attachment seemed extremely poor, with an absence of any real affection or feeling expressed by the child in relation to anyone in her family. When she was placed in her foster family she still had a dummy which she used for comfort. The foster mother replaced the dummy with a soft toy and the dummy was no longer used after a week.

Amelia had a regular programme of contact with her family of origin which included her brother, father and mother. This was supervised by her male social worker. The contact involved a range of family activities including swimming. During one of Amelia's group work sessions with the other girls, she revealed that she was feeling scared and that she didn't like "having to see" her family every week. This was pursued within the group session. Amelia said that when they went swimming, she would go into the changing room with her mother, as the supervisor and the other two members of her family were male. She was worried her mother would try to touch her again. The unsuitability of this contact activity was raised with the supervising social worker, and different activities were arranged. However, Amelia continued to complain about her contact sessions. Her complaints were ignored and she was compelled to see her family several times every week. This carried on for a considerable period of time. Her parents applied for an increase in contact, a removal of the supervision condition, and a request for rehabilitation, which they later withdrew.

In the assessment prior to the court hearing of the contact application, Amelia was adamant that she did not want contact with anyone in her family, not by phone, letter, photos, or cards. Amelia's parents agreed not to press for contact and argued that there was therefore no need for an order against contact. However, the order was necessary for Amelia as she felt it was the only way she would know she had been heard. The order was granted.

In both cases above, continued contact with the abusing parent serves only to keep the trauma alive for the child. The "no contact" option is meant to provide abused children with a breathing space to do reparative work, which will eventually give them greater strength and feelings of security to maintain their individual identity when coming face to face with members of their family of origin. If older children who have contact request to have no further contact, it is sometimes a repeat of previously unheard messages about how they are managing current contact. This is less likely to happen if children are encouraged to reassess their position regarding contact with their families of origin through regular case reviews. However, many will only feel able to confront their past when they are themselves adults.

Managing contact situations

If contact is mandated by law, it is important that primary caregivers understand their role in facilitating a positive experience for the child. In relation to this task, we have much to learn from the literature on divorce and separation. The transitional space between one home and the other is extremely important and often provides children with an opportunity to reorient themselves to the demands of the next context.

Direct handing over from one adult to the next is also important with some time given to ensure the child is settled and able to manage the separation. Sometimes it is in the child's interest for the primary caregiver to remain for the duration, rather than discreetly leave, as their presence makes it possible for the child to engage with parents or members of the family of origin but to also feel connected with their current family.

Developmental considerations need to be made as older adolescents clearly are more able to manage unsupervised contact without a primary caregiver present. However, it may also be important to them that they witness a connection being made between the adults responsible for them. If primary caregivers remain disconnected from the child's family of origin, it can be difficult to establish the necessary ongoing conversation with the child that will help reassess when contact should be changed. It also heightens the loyalty conflict for the child.

Case

> Onika was a 14-year-old girl of mixed parentage in a residential unit. She had been sexually abused by her white brother and by her mother's new husband, also white. She was very attached to her mother but could not live with her because of her mother's continuing attachment to her new husband despite his abuse of her daughter. Her mother was offered the possibility of coming to the unit to meet Onika. She took this up and regularly enjoyed meeting her daughter in the safety of the unit. However, when she arrived, she was frequently upset and distressed by her marital difficulties which meant that much of Onika's time was taken up with Onika caring for her mother rather than vice versa.
>
> To address this, one member of staff would greet Onika's mother,

settle her in to the contact room with a cup of coffee, and discuss with her any current difficulties she was experiencing, stressing how important it was for her to enjoy her time with Onika and not to burden Onika with her problems. This was done in a supportive way and allowed Onika's mother to collect herself and manage the contact with her daughter. For Onika, it demonstrated a connection to her mother and opened up the possibility of discussing her relationship with her mother not with her key worker as expected, but with the worker who helped to settle her mother in. The connection between the residential worker and the mother reinforced the mother's adult position, provided her with some individual support, and decreased her need to seek it from her daughter during their brief and limited contact time.

In situations involving abuse and supervision of contact, it is essential that the supervisor understands his or her role as protector. This includes accepting that abuse has happened and that an active role may be required during the contact time. Additionally children need to understand the role of the supervisor clearly. The following is the kind of message a child needs to hear from a contact supervisor: 'I am here to protect you and keep you safe. If you are feeling uncomfortable or scared you can talk to me about it either during or after the contact. If you need to leave or have the contact stopped, I can do this.'

It is important for the contact supervisor to recognise the need for action even if the child has not indicated any distress.

Case

Nathan, a four-year-old white boy, was having supervised contact with his father at his paternal grandparents' house. His father was alleged to have sexually abused him. Nathan had medical signs of having been sexually abused and had made clear verbal disclosures implicating his father but this was still being assessed, hence the supervised contact arrangements. The paternal grandparents did not think it was possible for their son to have sexually abused their grandson. Consequently, their role as protectors was already severely compromised. During one session, Nathan's dad built a tent in the living room for Nathan to play in. Both grandparents were in the living room while Nathan and his father played in the tent. When Nathan returned home to his mother's care he told his mother that Daddy had touched his private parts in the tent with nanny and granddad there. The paternal grandparents ought to have intervened and suggested that Nathan play in the tent alone with Daddy watching and contributing to the game at an unambiguous distance.

Other activities that frequently plague supervised contact sessions where abuse is an issue, is rather frantic rough and tumbles which can become sexualised in nature and certainly serve to excite the child, the giving of presents often quite lavish and sometimes against expressed wishes or instructions of both the court or the primary caregiver, and whispering. Other forms of secret language or non-verbal cues are impossible to monitor. However, supervisors need to trust their funny feelings and if they feel a situation is out of control or inappropriate they need to intervene and suggest an alternative way of having contact. This reinforces their authority in relation to the child and the parent as well as demonstrating the responsible exercise of authority necessary to effect safe caring.

Both children and parents can benefit from pre and post-contact discussions. They may then be able to use their time together not just to play, but sometimes to discuss questions or issues that have arisen which are best dealt with during contact sessions. This can include work on life story books. Many parents are not provided with any help or guidance on how to manage contact in a way that ensures the time is enjoyable and meaningful for children and their families.

Contact with siblings

Case

This case example involves a number of siblings raised in a family where emotional, physical and sexual abuse was part of the established family culture and probably had been for many generations. The seven siblings were removed from their family of origin and placed in six separate foster families. Initially there was regular supervised contact with the whole family group, which proved impossible to supervise. The children would engage in sexual activity with each other, by groping and grabbing at each others' genitals; the conversation was lewd and lascivious; the parents and step-parents would whisper with selected children passing money and gifts to them surreptitiously. The children would return to their respective placements very high and very sexualised.

Only one child, the eldest boy, did not attend contact meetings. He wanted to forget his past and get on with his new life. He said he found seeing his brothers and sisters extremely painful. In working with the next oldest sibling, a 12-year-old girl, it was clear that the children were encouraged to have sex with each other, and that older children were expected to "train" the younger children. The recommendation was for contact sessions with the parents to be suspended for a period of time, and for sibling contact to take place in pairs rather than with the whole group.

This enabled Nicola, the 12-year-old, to say she did not wish to see her father at all because he frightened her; nor did she wish to see her step-mother (who was also her aunt). She still wanted contact with her mother, who had also sexually abused her along with everyone else in the family. She wanted to see her full siblings but not her step siblings/ cousins. Alongside the contact sessions, a series of therapeutic meetings were arranged for dyads of siblings to explore, confirm and discuss their shared experience in their family of origin. During these sessions, it became clear that the younger siblings viewed Nicola as a perpetrator of abuse and found her frightening and contact with her profoundly disturbing. In one of these meetings, Nicola was then able to acknowledge that she had been sexually aggressive to her younger siblings and that she was sorry for this behaviour. She was also able to confirm that all the children had been abused by the various adults in their family. This helped some of the younger children to begin to move on in their recovery work.

This case illustrates the complex dynamics at work in families where abuse has occurred, which may often not be appreciated by outsiders, especially in relation to sibling groups. All of the children have made substantial progress in their respective placements, in part because they have been allowed to pursue their individual paths to recovery and the old family patterns have been necessarily disrupted. There could have been great pressure to place this sibling group together, without fully understanding that many sibling groups have been manipulated to establish abusive hierarchies and to abuse each other as part of their sibling relationship. Rivalries and hostilities may have been nurtured by parents as offering the best context for the abuse to continue.

Many alternative families find it most difficult to parent sibling groups, and some discover that the secret, sexually abusive relationships are kept alive by continuing abuse, sometimes involving their own children. In this way, the foster child's family of origin can dominate the foster family's own ethos.

For many adolescents contact with siblings is terminated by the parents, as a consequence of the young person's disclosure of sexual abuse. In these cases, I would like to see the law being used to secure continued contact, for often, the only way these young people are allowed to continue their relationships with significant others, including their siblings, is to retract their allegations of sexual and physical abuse.

In Nicola's family's case, it was possible to interpret contact arrangements flexibly, and to devise appropriate contact levels with key members of her family, whilst at the same time suspending contact with others. This required detailed consideration of the dynamics of the whole family of origin and special attention for each dyad within the family. So Nicola had supervised contact twice yearly with her mother. She has requested no more. She has had no contact with her father. She has not had any contact with her older brother for some years now, but had one therapeutic session with him during the early stages of her removal from her family which she found very helpful, as he was able to apologise for his abusive behaviour towards her and to confirm how terrible it had been when they were living at home. He was also able to disclose abuse that Nicola herself had been unable to describe. However, since then neither of them has wanted any more contact. Nicola has had no contact with her step-sisters/cousins. She has had no further contact with her younger sister or brother since both were seen with her in separate therapeutic sessions. In these sessions, it was Nicola who apologised and disclosed information to them about the abuse she had seen and experienced when living at home. Her sister, until that session, had steadfastly insisted that she had not experienced anything untoward in her family of origin.

Nicola continued to discuss her family of origin in her therapeutic work and on the occasions when she saw her mother she would ask her for information. Over time Nicola's mother has been unable to sustain her side of the contact arrangement, often arriving late and leaving early. At the most recent contact session she failed to turn up at all. Nicola remained relatively philosophical about this and, like many children who come from abusive families of origin, it is Nicola who occupies the parental position and demonstrates the greater maturity.

Nicola is now securely attached to her foster family despite having limited direct or indirect contact with her family of origin. She and her siblings have not opted for continuity of experience, precisely the opposite. They want to get away from their past and make new lives for themselves. This doesn't mean they don't know where they came from. But if you came from hell, wanting to experience a bit of heaven before you look back isn't too unreasonable, is it?

Summary and conclusions

I hope that this brief discussion of contact and the case examples help to open up the debate on contact to include the impact of trauma and abuse. Each case, while benefiting from the extensive body of research, still has to be considered on an individual basis. There is an urgent need to study "no contact" situations that appear to have had positive benefits for children and allowed them to get on with developmentally appropriate tasks, leaving the examination of their past to a later stage of development.

Out of sight does not mean out of mind. Children can be given help to make sense of their families of origin, without meeting them face to face. They may even want indirect contact to be kept from them until they are ready to deal with it, or to protect themselves from the hidden messages in cards and letters meant for only them. Parental love can be uncon-ditional, given with no expectation of return. Many women who relin-quished children at birth offer unconditional love in the cards or letters they may post or write in their heads; other parents separated from their children are also able to send their unconditional love. The benefits of straightforward communication and information can clearly outweigh any disadvantages. However, for children who have experienced physical and sexual abuse, parental love is often conditional: keep this secret, do as I say, I own you. Children should be protected from such messages, or where this is not possible, given the support to manage them.

If we do not provide children who have been abused with a secure base, preferably an alternative family experience from which to explore their past, then there is a danger that conditional love and care will almost certainly be preferred to no love or care at all. We need to ensure that we try to promote healthy attachments, to disrupt previously unhealthy attachments (by which I mean very sexualised and abusive contacts) and to facilitate the transformation of unhealthy attachments into healthy ones.

Continued contact with abusive families, rather than helping the child or young person move forward, can pull them back to their past. If contact is established, it should be in addition to current positive relationships. The natural curiosity and concern a parent may have for their child's future can be managed by the new adult caregivers who should not pass on the responsibility to the child. Even when children are anxious about the parents they have left behind, and wish contact to continue, it can sometimes be detrimental to the child's recovery, and reinforce the generational inversion of many abusing families where the child is parenting the parents. This is a developmentally inappropriate task.

We must have clearer guidelines on the exceptions to the rules of good practice which promote contact. Recognition of the different situations in which children enter the care system is needed. Often the child's history of abuse is such that continued contact is not in the child's interest and could possibly be dangerous.

References

1. Nissam R, and Simm M, 'Linking research evidence and practice in fostering work – the art of the possible', *Adoption & Fostering*, 18:4, BAAF, 1994.

2. Department of Health, *The Children Act 1989*, HMSO, 1991.

3. Thoburn J, *Success and Failure in Permanent Placement*, Avebury: Gower, 1989.

4. Fahlberg V, *Fitting the Pieces Together*, BAAF, 1988.

5. Ryburn M, *Open Adoption: Research, theory and practice*, Avebury: Gower, 1994.

6. Berry M, 'Adoptive parents' perceptions of and comfort with open adoption', *Child Welfare*, 72:3, 1993, USA.

7. See 5 above.

8. Lund, quoted in 5 above.

9. Phelan P, 'Incest and its meaning: the perspectives of fathers and daughters', *Child Abuse and Neglect*, 19:1, 1995.

The importance of contact for children with disabilities
Issues for policy and practice

Philippa Russell

Philippa Russell is the Director of the Council for Disabled children at the National Children's Bureau.

The importance of contact: the disability context

Over the past decade there have been major developments in terms of policy and practice for children with disabilities or special needs. Both the Children Act 1989 and the community care arrangements emphasise the importance of family based services and the need for comprehensive, flexible and accessible services to be widely available in the community. However, the same decade has seen the emergence of complex assessment systems and changes in the management of child health, education and social services. There is a growing emphasis upon quality in the commissioning of services but purchasing arrangements in a contract culture may be variable and difficult for consumers of services to understand. Major changes in the social security system have improved the financial situation of some families, but there is growing evidence that many families of children with disabilities suffer a "double jeopardy" with poor housing, low incomes, and additional financial costs because of caring.

It is estimated that there are around 360,000 children of sixteen or under with disabilities in the UK (about three per cent of the child population).[1] Of these children, all but 5,500 live in a family home for at least part of the time; 175,000 children are estimated to have severe or multiple disabilities.

Improved medical care – particularly in the neonatal period – has meant that more children with very severe disabilities are surviving much longer in childhood and beyond. This new group of children will require specialist services within the community if they are to remain within a family; the task of caring for them without adequate support may mean heavier demands upon substitute family placements, residential services, and short-term care over the coming decade. Because of their special needs, these children are more likely than their non-disabled peers to be placed at a considerable distance from their family home and they are less likely to be able to travel freely or communicate by phone or letter with family and friends in their home communities.

The OPCS study[2] notes that children with disabilities living away from home fall into discrete categories: 35 per cent were regarded by natural and substitute carers as having behaviour or health problems which were "too difficult" to cope with at home; 35 per cent experienced "problems at home", often reflecting a lack of appropriate level of support for the families concerned; 15 per cent of children were known to have been abused (almost certainly a considerable under-estimate). Forty five per cent of all caring families felt that their own health had been adversely affected by caring and that the health and well-being of siblings had also been adversely affected because of pressures on the parents.

The general shift away from residential services in many local authorities has led to an increased dependency upon residential education as a placement for children with disabilities, in particular for those with emotional or multiple disabilities: 16,500 children with special educational needs are currently attending residential schools, with the largest proportion of 8,000 children in schools for children with emotional and behavioural difficulties. There is also a clear trend for residential schools to offer 52 weeks a year boarding, often meeting the demands of social services departments which have shut residential homes but have not found family placements for the more challenging children with disabilities or special needs. In some instances children at residential schools are also using a variety of respite or holiday provision and are spending little time with their birth families. It is therefore necessary when considering issues relating to family links and contact, to ensure that the contribution of residential education is acknowledged, and that the educational as well as social services assessment arrangements are fully utilised in planning for children.

It is important to view disability in children in the context of a decade of major social change. The welcome shift away from institutional care (often within NHS provision) to "community care" has not always been matched by the development of good quality community based services. The principle of inclusion or integration still raises questions about how to meet very complex needs within mainstream services. Many generic children's services have found themselves ill equipped to deal with the often problematic and invariably inter-agency support services which disabled children require. Recent research[3,4,5] has clearly demonstrated that disabled children are more vulnerable than their peers to abuse and their welfare will require special vigilance.

Additionally, the United Kingdom is becoming an increasingly multi-cultural society, with very limited expertise in planning for disability within the new communities. The duties under the Children Act 1989, to take into account the 'ascertainable wishes and feelings of the child' have been particularly onerous with disabled children who may have limited communication, be distant from family and friends, and present real doubts about what constitutes "informed consent". Whilst partner-ships in assessment of children may be in their infancy, there has been an encouraging increase in services and projects which actively involve parents in their child's development and in care planning. However, these initiatives in turn clearly demonstrate that many parents of disabled children are too tired, have very limited information on which to base judgements, or there may be other life events or family problems which create barriers to participation. In some instances parents may actually doubt their own capacity to contribute to their child's needs.

Notwithstanding the growth of highly valued family support systems such as respite care, the OPCS survey[6] estimated that no more than four per cent of children had access to such a service. Additionally, the majority of children receiving good quality respite were young, did not have significant disabilities or behaviour problems, and tended to have active parents who knew local services and how to access them.[7,8] The identification of vulnerable families with disabled children *before* they break down presents a particular challenge to local authorities in implementing the general requirement of the Children Act.

Children with disabilities: contact as a placement priority
The Children Act 1989 provides a clear framework for ensuring that

children looked after by the local authority maintain contact with their family and community. Schedule 2 (para 15) gives local authorities the power to contribute to the costs of visits and contact and Schedule 2 (para 17) gives a little used (but potentially extremely important) power to the local authority to appoint an *independent visitor* if the child has little contact with parents and would benefit from an independent contact. Although the principle of contact has been widely endorsed, it is still occasionally seen as an obstacle to the permanent placement of children. However, even when a child (with or without a disability) is subject to a care order, the local authority must allow "reasonable contact" (Schedule 34 (1)) unless a court has decided otherwise. Parents and children (and the local authority) may appeal to the court for contact to be varied (ie. increased or decreased) and the local authority retains the right to deny contact for up to seven days, if this is felt to be a matter of urgency with regard to the safety of the child. Children with disabilities have no distinct status within the Children Act arrangements, but the arrangements may have certain consequences for them, precisely because they have disabilities; they may use different services from other children and they may have limited ability to express views on the plans made for them.

There is a considerable body of research which shows that contact with family members provides most children with a sense of belonging and continuity which it is very difficult for a local authority to recreate. Regular contact between children and birth families has a positive effect on their well being when living away from home. Additionally most "looked after" children will eventually go home and the process will be smoother if the links have been maintained.[9]

The revised *Assessment and Action Records*, published by the Department of Health in 1995, for children "looked after by the local authority" provide an important opportunity for building contact into assessment and review arrangements. The new records can help local authorities monitor the maintenance of contact between children and their families and provide an early warning system for those whose links are failing and where appropriate action should be taken. For the first time, a range of questions relating specifically to disability are included. Piloting of the forms suggests that they are equally relevant for children with disabilities who are not looked after by the local authority and that they provide a comprehensive framework for identifying, assessing, and meeting a wide range of needs. The "Looked after Children" Study Group, which supported the new materials, showed that contact remained a difficult area for all local authorities and that good quality and up-to-date information is essential for good practice, as situations change rapidly. For nearly half the children in the study (46 per cent), it was considered that more needed to be done to promote links with family members. For 13 per cent, contact was problematic because the parents did not measure up to expectations. Professionals considered that contact was detrimental to the child's well being in just over a quarter of the case studies. But about a third of the young people were unhappy with access and contact arrangements and almost all said they wanted more, not less, contact with family and friends.

Although the aim of contact might seem self-evident, it can be interpreted in a variety of different ways and be seen as important for a variety of reasons. Relationships with family members provide all children with a framework for interpreting experience, for learning to value themselves and to develop a sense of self-esteem, and for creating friendships with their peers. Children with disabilities have fewer informal opportunities to make friends and new contacts, and so the family is crucial in helping them to determine their place in the world and for acting as an advocate when required. Ward,[10] looking at the life experiences of children "looked after" and comparing them to a peer group of children in the community, notes that for the latter group:

> 'Support from members of the extended family was a major resource . . . and likely to be one that differentiated them from those in care or accommodation. Over 50 per cent of them saw not only grandparents but also aunts, uncles and other family members at least once a week. When families were dispersed, children were encouraged to maintain contact by letter or telephone. It was also common for children living in their own families to have a wide network of people other than family members to whom they could turn for help and advice. A friend's mother, their mother's friend or a neighbour they had known all their lives frequently took on this role.'

Replicating this network for disabled children and young people is hard work, but necessary, when even the use of the telephone may pose major difficulties and when the relatives in question may themselves hesitate about involvement, because of fears that they may not be competent to "manage" the disability adequately.

Some children with complex and multiple disabilities may appear to have very limited opportunities for (or even need of) contact.

Case

Elizabeth had been a very premature baby with many problems in the neonatal period. She is tube fed, doubly incontinent, is thought to have multi-sensory disabilities and has long periods of crying. Elizabeth's single mother could not manage to continue to care for her; suitable respite care was not available locally and Elizabeth's constant crying caused frictions with neighbours and within the family. The local paediatrician arranged for Elizabeth to spend time in a children's hospice, but the breaks were insufficient. Elizabeth moved into a small residential home eighty miles from her mother and other relatives. Initially she had no visitors; the family were fearful that any contact might mean their daughter returning home. They were also depressed and guilty that they could not care for her. Assistance with transport for visits was offered but not taken up. Elizabeth had two birthdays on her own, with only a birthday card and a small gift to remind everyone that she did have a family.

On Elizabeth's tenth birthday, a care worker sent a special invitation to her relatives. The invitation, to a tea party, made it plain that everybody wanted to see them; that the request was "without strings" and that, if necessary, the guests could be picked up by car. The care worker followed up the written invitation with a phone call, acknowledging it would be painful but stressing that Elizabeth did recognise people and that it would matter to her to see her family. The tea party was a tense occasion, but it was agreed that Elizabeth was looking well, that she did seem to recognise her family, and that she certainly enjoyed the attention, the music and her presents.

Elizabeth now sees her family every six weeks. Her grandmother sometimes takes her out in the car and thinks she might bring her home for a weekend soon. Everyone acknowledges that the residential home is "home" at least for the time being. But Elizabeth's care now builds in family contact; it is hoped that she will move nearer home when she moves on at eighteen and the staff have introduced a special "keep in touch" programme for families.

One young care worker commented as follows:

'I used to feel quite cross that families seemed to "dump" their children here. I felt it was wrong, they were just being selfish. Now I understand that "shared care" can be positive; that families have feelings too and I feel we, as staff, have gained from having regular visitors and realising just how hard parents can find coping on a day-to-basis with a severely disabled child. We realise that we as staff need training too in dealing with parents; many of them are old enough to be our own mothers and fathers! But we build "contact" into the planning system and we look for nice activities which can be shared. I used to feel that children like Elizabeth didn't really know anyone. Now I know they do – but friendships and family need nurturing when you can't communicate and everybody feels so guilty all the time.'
(personal communication)

The importance of contact: the role of the "independent listener"
For all those children with disabilities who use short or longer term residential or substitute family care, or who attend residential schools, there are major issues about both creating and sustaining contact. Because a placement may reflect a long period of stress and sometimes unrelieved care in the family, and because such a placement may be associated with both grief and guilt if the family could no longer cope, relationships may become fragile or indeed break down altogether. The OPCS survey[11] found that family contact when disabled children were in residential care for over two years, began to decline exactly as it did for other children. In some instances this reflected problems in travelling to a distant placement; in others the parents fear that they would be expected to resume full-time care without sufficient support and some families sense that the child is better cared for by "experts"

and that the family has no ongoing role to play.

There has been no systematic review of contact arrangements for disabled children away from home. Indeed Sir William Utting,[12] commenting on children "in public care", noted that very little was known about residential care for disabled children and that there was an urgent need to increase understanding of this group of children's additional and special needs.

A particular cause of concern with regard to children with disabilities "looked after" by the local authority (or in residential education) is the difficulties they may experience in sharing any concerns or anxieties about their lives. The Social Services Inspectorate (SSI), in a report on the welfare of children in boarding schools[13] refers to "independent listeners" (Section 6.23), and emphasises the importance of all children having access to both a private telephone line and '*adults, independent of the school, who have a role as independent listeners, counsellors . . . there is a delicate balance to be struck. They should not be complete strangers . . . yet they must be seen to be divorced as far as possible from the school hierarchy. Finding people to fulfil both of these specifications will be difficult.*'

The same report echoes recommendations made in a report published by the Gulbenkian Foundation,[14] which also stresses the need for independent visitors (local authorities already having powers to make such appointments under the Children Act) for children who are living at some distance from family and friends and who may *not* achieve an independent voice without a facilitator external to the service within which they are placed.

The SSI suggests that the role of "independent listener" can be fulfilled by a range of people in addition to professionals: '*interested parents, volunteers or other persons who have a professional interest in counselling or pastoral care*' might also provide support for children away from home. The same report stresses – with equal relevance for children "looked after" – that access to the telephone is of great importance. It also reminds us that access to the telephone is more than physical access. Children who have to ask permission, who can be overheard, or whose disability makes independent access difficult, may simply not wish to use the telephone; or conversations may be so "edited" that they have little significance. Sometimes carers may themselves limit conversations because they fear that children who are "homesick" or "having a temporary problem", will merely cause anxiety to parents or other family members. But problems shared are proverbially halved and the SSI further reminds readers of the availability of independent helplines (such as Childline) not only when children have significant anxieties but also at times when children need: *'an unseen and friendly voice to share concerns and discuss problems and worries.'*

Although telephone lines may seem a poor substitute for physical contact, they (and other communication aids) may be very valuable when children are placed at considerable physical distance from home.

Case

Jenny, a ten-year-old girl with spina bifida, was placed in a residential school when ten years old. Her single parent mother had mental health problems and Jenny's physical care had been seriously neglected. The school was a success, but Jenny (unlike most of her peers) had no home to go to in the school holidays. The local authority arranged a family placement but because of Jenny's access needs (she was totally dependent upon a wheelchair), the placement was two hundred miles from her home town. Jenny had two older brothers, both in their first jobs. She also had a grandmother of whom she was very fond. None of them could visit her at school or in the holidays and none were very active letter writers. Jenny was becoming more and more isolated and there was some concern that family contact could break down altogether. Jenny's own wishes surfaced at a review meeting and it was agreed to set up a contact plan. The contact plan had three specific aims, namely:

● To ensure that Jenny retained regular contact with her brothers and grand-mother (and through them with friends and neighbours) so that she could return home when leaving school.

● To encourage Jenny's family to include her in any special family events and to feel positive (and not threatened) by increased contact. It was recognised that Jenny's brothers were frightened that Jenny might come home and that they would be expected to care for her in their mother's absence.

- To identify a variety of strategies for maintaining contact, ranging from phone calls and letters to visits.

The plan was made in full partnership with Jenny, with a "no blame" approach if some of the proposed activities did not work. Firstly, Jenny was enabled to phone her brothers and grandmother once a week. Initially she was very shy and said she had "nothing to say". The school staff and her family carer both helped her to make a note of the week's special events, her "news", so that the conversation had some life to it. Jenny was also encouraged to keep her own diary with family birthdays and special events so that she could send cards, phone and generally feel involved.

Secondly, Jenny was reminded to write regular letters and to send periodic tapes to her grand-mother, who was losing her sight. She also wrote regularly to her mother in hospital. Jenny's family had indicated right from the start that they could not afford to visit either the school or the family placement. Both were expensive and inconvenient journeys and would have been difficult to carry out as a day visit. Social services therefore agreed to organise Jenny's travel for periodic visits to and from the grandmother's home. The visits are planned carefully (usually linked to a birthday or special event at school) and have been very successful. The school has been sufficiently impressed to allocate two rooms for visitors and to ask a number of the sponsoring local authorities if they would fund regular family visits.

One year on, Jenny's programme is working well. Her contact has been well planned and is carefully supported. It involves investment in travel costs for her brothers to visit the school and family placement – and for Jenny to go home to visit her grandmother. But Jenny has retained contact. For one year there were no visits to or from her mother because of the severity of her mental health problems. Jenny had expressed considerable anxiety about her mother, but had been reluctant to visit her (in part because of her own fear of hospitals). Jenny is very clear that she does not wish to return to live with her mother. The contact is being re-established slowly as there is little chance of Jenny and her mother living together again in the foreseeable future.

Maintaining family links: putting policy into practice

The Care of Children: Principles and Practice in Regulations and Guidance published by the Department of Health in 1992 sets out key principles for maintaining contact for all children (with or without disabilities). These principles include recognition that:

- Parents should be expected and enabled to retain their responsibilities and to remain as closely involved as is consistent with their child's welfare, even if the child cannot live at home temporarily or permanently.
- Siblings should not be separated . . . unless this is part of a well thought out plan based on each child's needs.
- Family links should be actively maintained through visits and other forms of contact. Both parents are important even if one of them is no longer in the family home and fathers should not be overlooked. A parent's inability to sustain contact should not be assumed to be an indication of lack of interest and concern. For some families, visiting is painful and difficult.
- Wider families matter – especially siblings and grandparents.
- Continuity of relationships is important and attachments should be respected, sustained and developed.

Case

Marcus, a young man of twelve with a profound hearing loss and well controlled epilepsy, is an example of how such principles may be translated into practice. Marcus has attended a residential school since the age of eight. His holidays were spent mainly with his grand-parents, as his parents found his special needs and those of his younger siblings very difficult to balance. Marcus moved from his residential school to a local day school at the age of twelve. He moved schools again when his parents failed to cope with his return home; his grandparents felt too old to have him and the only family placement appropriate to his communication needs was in the next county. Marcus deteriorated rapidly. He was depressed; his communication was poor; his school felt he was significantly under-achieving. He alleged bullying at school, he was also frequently named as a bully himself and was unpopular with his fellow pupils. His parents felt that a return to residential education was the only option.

A care plan was attached to his family placement, which put great emphasis upon Marcus' views of the world and upon his personal relationships, which seemed very infirm. Marcus preferred to use BSL (British Sign Language) and a social worker was identified who could communicate with him without difficulty. It emerged that although Marcus liked his family placement, he desperately missed his grandfather, who he feared might die while he was away. He missed his parents and his younger siblings, but accepted that 'mum can't afford the bus fares for them all to visit me out here'. He said he would like to go home regularly and he was worried that in his absence, the family might get rid of their dog, to whom he was very attached. The local authority agreed that it would pay the travel expenses for the family to visit Marcus regularly – and to meet his teachers at his new school. They also agreed to consider regular home visits for Marcus, subject to his parents' agreement. The visits were established, but Marcus continued to be a lonely child and to be periodically in trouble for bullying and teasing younger children. His school work remained poor and his head of year at his comprehensive school felt that he had "very low self esteem" and that he was a "natural victim".

Marcus's foster carers were similarly becoming aware of his anxiety and about the escalation of various troubled behaviours. It was decided to involve Marcus in an open discussion about what he felt about his previous life and whether there were people or activities which should be carried into his present one. Discussions revealed that Marcus had felt very positively about his residential school (where he had done well) and that he particularly missed two friends whom he had known for four years and whom he saw as "almost brothers". He felt he could say "anything, just anything" to them. With some hesitancy about disrupting his present education, the social services department contacted the school and asked if Marcus might perhaps visit his old friends. The school (which has a national remit) has taken the request seriously and now has regular "reunions" and other special events to enable pupils to return and to sustain old friendships. An important spin-off of this renewed contact is that one of Marcus's ex-teachers has visited him at his new school and has provided a range of information which had got "lost" in the transfer.

Although the idea might seem trivial to adults with little interest in pets, Marcus genuinely wanted to retain contact with his dog. The importance of pets for security and continuity is mirrored by the author's experiences, when taking part in a live Blue Peter programme on the Children Act. The children highlighted keeping beloved pets, attending the same school, and being able to practice their religion as three key factors in placement planning. All have implications for managing and developing meaningful contact.

As a result of planned contact arrangements, Marcus's birth and his substitute parents have become more involved in his education. Marcus has an Individual Education Plan (as required under the new arrangements in the Code of Practice[15] and both sets of families now help him to work on a number of educational objectives. One has been to improve his social relationships in his new school. As Ward notes[16] discussing the work of the Department of Health's initiative on assessing outcomes in child care,[17] 'one of the key principles of "looking after" children is that parenting is a process which is shared between individuals and the community'. In Marcus's case, that "community" includes the deaf community, with its own culture and language and its capacity to provide some very specialist support. The local authority responsible for Marcus is now reviewing its policy on the appointment of independent visitors for children with very specific needs relating to their disabilities and acknowledging that some disabled children will need informed, confident and expert support and contact from outside the local authority's usual networks.

Ward[18] and Jackson[19] note the significance of school changes for children in public care. Ward notes that 43 per cent of children who changed addresses three times or more had also changed schools (often more than once) and these children featured disproportionately in the group of children who had been excluded from school. For children like Marcus, with special educational needs, the new arrangements in the Code of Practice and the 1993 Education Act permit much more active partnerships between social services and the local education authority. But such partnerships are unlikely to occur unless good working relationships are encouraged between a whole range of people in children's lives as well as contact with the child. One important message with regard to the "contact plan" developed for Marcus is that some of his contacts in the specialist schools and services he used have provided new opportunities for the future. Marcus's former school has put the local authority in touch with a leisure group for deaf people and Marcus has made some new friends. The partnership between the two schools has meant that Marcus's educational opportunities have improved. He enjoys the renewed contact with his former friends and writes to them between visits. His parents feel more relaxed and his home visits are more successful. It is possible that he will return home for a second attempt at resettlement within the next few months.

The role of the independent visitor

Paragraph 17 of Schedule 2 of the Children Act places a duty on local authorities to appoint an independent visitor in regard of any child they are looking after if they believe it would be in a child's best interests and certain conditions are satisfied. Chapter 6 (section 6.2) of *The Children Act 1989 Regulations and Guidance: Residential Care*[20] states that:

> *'The need for such an appointment arises where communication between the child and his parent or a person who is not a parent but has parental responsibility has been infrequent or where he has not visited or been visited by his parents or a person who is*

not a parent but has parental responsibility during the preceding 12 months.'

The same guidance notes that children should be involved in choosing who they would like as an independent visitor and that issues relating to religion, culture, race and language should also be considered. Some children may wish to have a contact who is more like an elder sibling, or who may also have had experience of public care or who may come from the same religious or ethnic background. Others may wish for a much older person, like a surrogate grandparent. Local authorities have the power to appoint relatives directly and where distance and cost have been the main contributing factors to contact breaking down, such an arrangement would be entirely practical. The Department of Health notes that recruitment needs to be handled carefully. Ideally independent visitors can offer a reasonable time commitment but the need for special skills or interests may make some short-term appointments inevitable. The visitor's *'personal qualities, ability to communicate with children; commitment and interest in children's welfare'* will be paramount. But in practice (notwithstanding a strong plea from the Gulbenkian Foundation's report, *One Scandal too Many,*[21] on safety issues for children with disabilities living away from home), the role of the independent visitor has been little exploited. There are widespread fears about the risk of abuse and about a lack of clarity in some aspects of the role.

For children with disabilities, the functions of the independent visitor remain a potential resource, not least in creating and sustaining "bridges" between children placed at a distance from the family home, since easy and cheap travel for visits are a rare option.

Case

Khalida has severe learning difficulties and epilepsy as the result of a head injury when she was two years old. She fell from a balcony in her parents' over-crowded and poorly maintained inner-city flat. She is fourteen years old and the oldest of six children. When she was seven, her mother became very ill after the birth of a child and Khalida started to use extended respite care. The use of respite care (in three different settings provided by health, social services and the voluntary sector) escalated until Khalida's mother died when she was twelve. Khalida then spent a year in a residential school and has since moved to what is hoped will be a permanent family placement.

Khalida's behaviour, because of her injury, is often very challenging and four family placements have broken down. Khalida's expressive language is poor and her English limited but she is making progress in her present school. However, the current (and so far most successful placement) is in another urban area, 80 miles from her family home. In principle, Khalida's natural family want to work closely with her placement, the school and all other agencies to ensure an integrated care management approach to meet her needs. In practice, the reality is different. There are poor Bengali translation or interpretation facilities in the new authority and Khalida's parents are in any event very nervous about official meetings. Her mother had travelled very little and the aunt, who has arrived from Bangladesh to care for the children, finds partnership very difficult. The family feels considerable shame that Khalida is cared for by outsiders – especially by social services – and worry that her care and her diet may not be appropriate. Because of the lessening number of visits, Khalida's own awareness of family and community was fading. Time and financial resources had reduced social work input and there was a real risk that Khalida could slip out of contact with her family and lose her connection with her community.

The local authority in question decided that an independent visitor would be valuable, firstly, in helping Khalida retain a sense of her own identity; secondly, to provide a resource for her new family, school and those supporting her on issues relating to race, culture and religion; and thirdly, to encourage her natural family to continue to play a positive role in her life. An independent visitor was appointed from the local Bangladeshi community, with the advice of local organisations. Chandra is a former teacher, is well known within her community, and has a daughter of the same age as Khalida. The local authority has agreed to pay for all travel costs and also for Khalida to be escorted back to London for "special events" such as religious or family festivals. Although many independent visitors would not choose to do so, Chandra periodically attends parents' evenings and reviews at Khalida's school. When possible, she brings Khalida's father and aunt and acts as interpreter so that they understand what and how their daughter is learning. The LEA within which Khalida is now being educated has asked Chandra if she would consider becoming a "named person" to both the substitute family and Khalida's own family. "Named persons" are appointed under the 1993 Education Act to provide independent advice and support for parents whose children are going through statutory assessment of special educational needs or for children themselves.

Chandra's involvement has led to improved contact with all the family. Her confidence in dealing with educational matters and in working directly with children has meant that she is not deterred by Khalida's occasionally very difficult behaviour. The foster carers have been reassured by her support and advice (and praise) for keeping Khalida's own sense of identity and culture alive. Despite the regular visits home, it seems unlikely that Khalida will return permanently to East London. At fourteen, important plans have to be made about her future, in particular, a transition plan as required under the 1993 Education Act and Code of Practice. Chandra's role will continue to be of great significance during this period of change. Trusted by all parties, she has demonstrated how effective the role can be and, furthermore, how the use of independent visitors may be one of the few resources available to local authorities, who have no option but to place children from a range of multicultural backgrounds in localities where there is no existing body of knowledge about their needs and aspirations.

Conclusion

Children with disabilities lead complex lives. The greater their levels of need, the more likely they will be to be placed at considerable distance from the family home for short or longer term care. Many children use multiple services, with mixtures of generic and specialist education, health care and social services support. Maintaining contact with family and community often means keeping in touch with very many individuals or services who actually know a child. The majority of children with a disability will grow and develop and make progress. But the majority will also continue to need support even into adult life. Hence contact is not only about short-term relationships. It is about constantly checking and reviewing personal and professional contacts and ensuring these are not lost.

An important point for reflection is that many disabled children read and write with difficulty, their speech may be poor, and their physical access to telephones limited. Establishing and supporting contact between children with disabilities and their families requires imagination, creativity and patience. Touch and smell might be used, for instance, if sight or hearing are impaired. Records matter too, with names, addresses, phone numbers and photographs to ensure that personal histories are not lost. Many disabled children now have life story books (even if they spend short times away from home). The use of video, radio cassettes, drawings and letters are all important ways of describing lives and people. One child with a degenerative metabolic disease and high levels of disability (frequently using a distant residential short-term care placement) has made a video with his siblings of "our lives", recording people, places, pets, leisure activities and favourite personal possessions. As one young woman[22] in a self advocacy group for young people with learning difficulties commented:

> *'When you have a disability, people see you as a problem first. You're always a special need. They don't ask you about your mates, the people who matter. People are always going away. If you can't read, you can't find where they've gone. There are lots of people in our lives who can tell you about the good times, what we can do – not what we can't. But often no-one knows who the people are. What we need is a people map! Then nobody would miss out!'*

Kayleigh's comments about the "people map" (or contact plan) sum up the spirit of active contact planning and the importance of recognising, consolidating and using the natural networks of children. For children with disabilities, "people mapping" and valuing all those other people in children's crowded lives will be an essential ingredient for eventual reintegration into their family or for staying connected if they remain away from home.

References

1. Office of Population and Census Surveys (OPCS), *OPCS Survey of Disability in the UK, Report 3: Prevalence of Disability among Children Report 6, Disabled Children, Services Transport and Education*, HMSO, 1989.

2. See 1 above.

3. Kennedy M, 'Overcoming Myths: The abused disabled child', *Concern*, Summer 1990, 5–7, National Children's Bureau, 1990.

4. Russell, P, *Children with Disabilities*, in Owen, H, and Pritchard J (eds), *Good Practice in Child Protection: A manual for professionals*, Jessica Kingsley Publishers, 1994.

5. Westcott, H, *The Abuse of Children and Adults with Disabilities*, NSPCC, 1993.

6. See 1 above.

7. Robinson C, *Assessing Quality in Services for Disabled Children under the Children Act 1989*, Norah Fry Research Centre, University of Bristol, 1994.

8. Russell P, *Access to the System*, in Mittler P, and Mittler H (eds), *Family Support for Parents of Disabled Children*, Lisieux Press, 1995.

9. Ward H, *Looking after Children: Research into practice*, HMSO, 1995.

10. See 9 above.

11. See 1 above.

12. Utting W, *Children in Public Care: A review of residential child care*, HMSO, 1993.

13. Social Services Inspectorate (SSI), *Welfare of Children in Boarding Schools: A Practice Guide*, HMSO, 1992.

14. Newell P, *One Scandal too Many,* Gulbenkian Foundation, 1994.

15. Department for Education, *The Code of Practice on the Identification and Assessment of Special Educational Needs*, DFE, 1994.

16. See 9 above.

17. Department of Health, *Patterns and Outcomes in Child Placement: Messages from current research and their implications*. HMSO, 1991.

18. See 9 above.

19. Jackson S, *Educating Children in Residential and Foster Care*, Oxford Review of Education, 1994.

20. Department of Health, *The Children Act 1989 Regulations and Guidance: Residential Care*, HMSO, 1992.

21. See 14 above.

22. Russell P, and Wertheimer A, *Something to Say: Group work with young women with disabilities*, National Children's Bureau, forthcoming publication 1995.

8 'Hello mother, hello father'
Contact in residential care

Phil Youdan

Phil Youdan is the Principal Development Officer of the Residential Care Unit at the National Children's Bureau.

Throughout the twenty or so years that I have been associated with the residential care of children and young people, the often repeated comment – 'if it wasn't for the parents, everything would be alright' – has haunted me. When I was a residential worker, I can recall that on more than one occasion, the delivery of these immortal lines came from my lips. Not out of any deep-rooted malice, nor did I really believe in the sentiments being expressed by this thoughtless cliché; my delivery was born from frustration. The frustration of having once more to witness a child's disappointment at a "no-show" by a parent or relative. Frustration, that as the child's carer, I worked within a system that kept my communication with the parents to a minimum. Frustration, that in many cases, despite my best attempts, I could not emulate the bond which exists between a child and their natural parents, regardless of the child's past experiences, disappointments and outward anger – an anger which all too often appeared to be singularly focused upon me. I was the person who had cried with the children, nursed them when they were sick, cooked for them, shared jokes, and protected them, not to mention the numerous times I had represented them at the countless meetings called to "shape" their future development, but I was nevertheless the innocent recipient of rage deserved by others. Did they not appreciate that my purpose for being there was to save them, make things better and set them on course for a more fulfilling life, giving them a "fresh start"?

Although not always visible to me in my daily dealings with their child, the parents nevertheless posed an undeniable threat to my authority and to my professional ability to repair their "damaged child", and above all, to my need for an uncomplicated and uncompromising relationship with the child. Parental interference or partnership meant that instead of being the "captain" I was demoted to the role of "co-pilot."

This selfish, isolationist view of the residential task may, on first inspection, appear to be somewhat alarming. In my defence, and in order to avoid outright condemnation from my peers, the views expressed above, although based upon personal experience, are intended to share with the reader the more negative feelings which, if left unchecked, can prevent the successful involvement of parents, whatever their individual circumstances or motives, in the care and upbringing of their child or children. This "us and them" attitude, which still exists in some residential settings, affects not only the relationship between the residential worker and parents and others who may be important to the child, it may also impede the liaison with teachers, social workers and other professionals.

The "isolationist" view is deeply rooted in the history of institutional care in this country and the "poor law approach" to welfare, which perpetuated the notion that recipients of welfare should be grateful for the help they receive, regardless of the personal or emotional cost. This insistence upon gratitude was still very much in evidence when I first entered the care profession. I can recall being an "uncle" to a group of forty children and young people. On public outings many onlookers commented about one so young being an "uncle" to so many, particularly in view of the fact that the children and young people were drawn from a range of different cultures and racial backgrounds.

The view that permeated the state care of children until after the Second World War was the "fresh start" approach. Contact with children in care by their families was actively discouraged.[1] This approach was also supported by the voluntary, mainly religious, child care agencies. Dr Barnardo himself, for example, did not try to hide his attitude to parents, stating openly that 'parents are my chief difficulty everywhere; so are relatives generally . . . because I take from a very low class".[2] It was this prevailing attitude, which within Barnardo's own lifetime, led to the "forced" emigration of 100,000 children, co-ordinated by the various child care agencies in existence at the time. This practice continued until the early 1960s. It would be unreasonable to hold Barnardo personally responsible for this "fresh start approach" or to judge him and his peers solely by the standards of today. They were reacting to the prevailing social and economic climate and the belief that the best way to help children was to rescue them from the deprivation and poverty that existed. They were not concerned with bringing about social change. Such was the strength of these ideas that despite a relaxation of the social attitudes which accompanied the "poor law", it was not until the Children Act 1948, that an obligation to work towards rehabilitation first appeared in legislation.

Greg Kelly[3] cites the emergence of Bowlby's theories of maternal deprivation and the incorporation of these theories within the newly formed courses for child care officers, coupled with the birth of the welfare state, the death of the poor law, and some attempts to bury the attitudes which underpinned it, as important benchmarks. Together these developments challenged the earlier held beliefs which had remained virtually intact since the emergence of the Victorian charities.

However, it was not until the Children Act 1989 that the importance of parental contact with children in care was finally acknowledged, and attempts were made to redress the balance and deficits of previous legislation. The Act provided for the first time a statutory presumption in favour of contact, which can only be overridden, in the long term, by an order denying contact, provided it can be proved that to do so is in the "best interest of the child."

Models of contact

Simon Jolly,[4] lecturer in law at the University of Nottingham, offers up four models of contact, which he characterises as the rehabilitation, continuity, disruption and deterrence models.

Rehabilitation model

The "rehabilitation" approach uses the function of contact to facilitate the resumption of care by a natural parent. Contact is seen as a way of reducing the upsets and distress which may be caused when a child moves from one carer to another, a process which can also involve changing home, school and friends. This model is also a means by which the stress associated with a return to the family can be reduced. In situations where concerns have been raised about the parents' capacities, contact can be used to assess their abilities and to teach "caring skills".

However, when residential workers do not see contact as a means to promote rehabilitation, but purely as an end in itself, then there is a danger that the aims will be undermined. I can recall a situation where plans were made for the parents to share in the care of their child within the children's home, as a prerequisite to the child's return to the family. The plan was that the parents would cook a meal, play with the child and help settle him into bed. Unfortunately, some staff felt the presence of the parents was "disruptive" and an unnecessary extra burden upon their busy work load. Instead of being helped to spend time with their child, the parents were often left unattended except for the occasional 'would you like another cup of tea' and 'don't worry, we will sort their dinner out'. Reports on the quality and use made of the contact stated that the parents were unable to 'motivate themselves sufficiently to care for their child's needs, although they seem to enjoy the contact and are always on time'. Hence, the potential for using contact to help the parents learn was lost and was suppressed for the "greater good" of the institution.

Continuity model

The "continuity model" is close to the idea of the "kinship defenders". The loss of a primary carer can be a traumatic experience for a child. It can lead to feelings of rejection and anger and low esteem: 'If my mum and dad really loved me, they wouldn't put me in a home, would they?' It can also affect the relationship with the substitute carers, as the child may hold back from investing in new relationships, fearing that the past may repeat itself. It is not uncommon for children and young people in residential homes to challenge the motives of their carers: 'you only do it for the money' can be difficult to counter, particularly if you are keen to get away at the end of a shift, on time, to your family. Continued contact is considered important for promoting children's welfare and for enhancing their sense of identity. Continuity provides crucial links with the past and helps to encourage parents to retain their sense of responsibility towards their child. In my own residential experience, I met many parents who expressed "distrust" of social workers, perceiving them as the person who "broke up their family" or "took them to court". They did not view the residential workers in the same light and consequently they would often share information about their child more readily with us. Why a child would not eat certain foods, or sleep on their own, or had particular bedtime rituals – these are items of important information which offered continuity. Significantly it was information which they had kept back from the social worker for fear of being judged "bad parents".

Disruption model
The "disruption model" states that the "social" carers should replace the "natural parents"; this view is perhaps more applicable to children placed in foster care or for adoption. It is argued that to continue contact will only confuse the child and create uncertainty about the role of both the "natural" and "social parent". In residential care, the "disruption" argument is sometimes used to prevent involvement from parents who are perceived by staff as difficult. The parents who constantly phone or visit, wanting to know how their child is and who constantly appear critical of the staff's "parenting" abilities, may find themselves labelled "disruptive", in an attempt to curtail their unwarranted "interference".

I vividly remember an African Caribbean mother who, following every contact visit would ask to speak to me, the homes manager, about "your bloody white staff" and their indifference to the needs of herself and her children. Her complaints to staff were often abusive and delivered at the top of her voice. Initially staff put her behaviour down to her being "strange", and several staff members suggested that her access be terminated, as it was unsettling for the children. Discussions with the children themselves revealed that although they found their mum's behaviour embarrassing at times, mainly because of staff comments afterwards, they nevertheless looked forward to her visits, or as one of them said, 'At least it shows she cares, not like some of the kids here'. Following this confirmation by the children, I tackled mum about her behaviour and the reasons for these "outbursts". This gave her the opportunity to explain that her anger was a direct result of having grown up in care, and of having been looked after by white carers who failed to acknowledge her race and culture. Although prevented from caring for her own children, she was determined that they would not suffer her experience. She also said, 'If I wasn't difficult, would you listen and make sure your staff pays attention to the needs of my children?'

The "disruption argument" may also be used by residential workers on occasions to justify the termination of contact between parent and child on the grounds that the child is unable to settle and therefore progress. An example would be the attempts to curtail the barrack room lawyer, whose continued taunts of 'you're not my mum, so you can't tell me what to do' can be interpreted as a threat to the authority of individual staff members. Staff's argument for terminating contact is born out of frustration with the child and the need for compliance; it has little do with any feelings of "confusion"or "uncertainty" the child may have.

Deterrence model

The "deterrence model" claims that prospective carers are often unwilling to care for a child unless the bonds with natural parents have been severed – the so called "clean break" approach. Although primarily concerned with adoption, the argument can spill over into the residential care field, particularly establishments which prepare children for long-term foster care or adoption. The argument not only goes against the recommendations of research[5] it also fails to acknowledge the child's own historical experience and memory of their family. Inherent in this approach is the assumption that work can be done to either diminish the child's knowledge or to "package" the past in a way which will endorse the decision to make a "clean break". This leads to the risk of social workers and carers concealing information about the child's family which might interfere with the "break", and to little or no effort being made to seek other family members who, if approached, could offer a home or support to the child or young person.

The concealment of information can have far reaching effects beyond childhood. For example, the concealment of a child's family history may mean that important medical or personal information is lost. This could matter in later life, particularly if there is a family history of hereditary illness, which may skip generations or be gender related. Concealment also raises serious moral issues: should decisions about a person's earlier years ignore their future rights and abilities as an adult to make informed decisions? The separation of siblings, for instance, may deprive the individuals concerned of a sense of family; this in turn can lead to a sense of isolation and lack of identity. I was once confronted by an angry young man, who as a child had lived in a home in which I was a young staff member. I remembered him with affection as a child with whom I got on well, because of the "trust" that existed between us. Now, as an adult, he felt "betrayed", because I had colluded with the "system" and had not shared with him that he had a brother and sister who had been placed in foster care in another part of the country. My collusion was a consequence of the prevailing practice at the time, but nevertheless, this young man brought home to me that as a social worker, I need to be aware of how my actions or decisions, however well intended, can have adverse long-term effects.

These four models build upon the two value positions of contact identified by L Fox[6] who labels them as "kinship defenders" and the "society as parent protagonist". Both schools of thought place importance on contact when there is a prospect of the child's return to the "natural" family. However, when the opportunity for rehabilitation is removed, those adhering to the view of "society as parent protagonist" argue that any continuity of contact greatly reduces the chances of finding long-term alternative solutions. The "kinship defenders", on the other hand, maintain that continued contact with birth parents may still remain beneficial to the child's development. A longitudinal study by Fanshel and Shinn[7] found that children in long-term care who had received visits, showed significantly greater gains in verbal IQ scores, and were less defiant and less tense than children without contact. Yet a study by Jane Rowe and Lydia Lambert[8] of 2,812 children in statutory and voluntary care, reported that only 18 per cent saw one parent at least once a month and forty one per cent of all children in the study had no parental contact at all. The major cause for this apparent parental disinterest was, they felt, a direct consequence of the fact that 'some individual social workers and a few whole agencies were inclined to disparage parents' capabilities and interest and kept them out of the picture'.

Obstacles to contact
Studies undertaken by Bullock et al[9] and Berridge[10] suggest several possibilities why maintaining contact between the parents and the child in residential care, may run into difficulties and lead to "drift". Firstly, residential establishments work most effectively with groups; the

individual needs of the child become secondary to the need to maintain the compliance of the group. Hence parents are not invited at meal times, or the child is faced with the dilemma of having to choose between a group activity or a visit from mum and dad. The tendency of some homes to focus solely on the needs of the "group" can lead to what I call the "hello mother, hello father" scenario. Children are "encouraged" to keep up contact until the contact interferes with the needs of the group. So if sport is on the timetable, contact will have to wait. It is not unheard of for staff to "persuade" a child to be involved in an activity on the promise that 'you can see mum and dad later; anyway, if you don't go the others can't either.' This group mentality can, in turn, be internalised by the children and young people and if left unchecked, can lead to over-reliance upon the group to the detriment of their family relationship.

This group approach can also have adverse consequences if children have come into care as a direct result of their relationships and position within the family. The non-specialisation of many children's homes means that individual members of the group do not necessarily share a common set of membership criteria, other than residence. A collective approach for all endangers individually tailored case plans and the 'problems faced by the children to stay in contact with their families may be glossed over in attempts to provide the best for all'.[11]

Secondly, because residential care takes place away from the family, contact may have a low priority. This can lead to families feeling excluded from the care of their children. This was reported by R Thorpe[12] who found that many of the parents she interviewed felt cut off from the lives of their children, did not feel encouraged to maintain contact, and some felt they were being "judged and condemned" as bad parents. Very few experienced social workers as "potentially helpful". This exclusion of parents is often compounded by the lack of any planned and meaningful interaction with the residential staff. Despite the attempts of the Children Act 1989 to clarify and simplify the issue of parental responsibility, parents may remain uninvolved with their children in residential care, not through disinterest but through poor planning and practice. By focusing solely on the child, social workers and carers support the view that the child is the "problem" and so overlook the child's relationship with the family. Residential care which allows distancing between children and their families can have further detrimental long-term effects. The alienation of a family and their lack of involvement in the upbringing of their child, can result in valuable family history being lost or withheld.

Managing contact between children and their families does require considerable skill on the part of residential social workers. They need to be able to help parents overcome feelings of guilt and inadequacy arising from their having to share responsibility for their children. At the same time, children may need considerable help in coming to terms with the anger and anxieties they experience because they have been removed from their family; feelings which will be even more complicated if they have been abused by their family. Although outwardly children may not display anger towards their parents or appear apathetic to their situation, their behaviour in their new environment may be directly related to the enforced separation. The realisation that the family can operate without them only serves to deepen their sense of loss and rejection. It is therefore essential that parents are encouraged to keep children informed about what is happening at "home" and that links with their community are not lost.

Good practice indicators

● Information for parents, children and referring agencies should include details about the arrangements for contact, the name of the staff member who has particular responsibility for the child, the name of the supervisor, an out of hours telephone number, what role the parents will continue to have in respect of their child, how these arrangements are to be monitored and reviewed, and how the agency's complaints procedure works.

● Parents should be kept informed on a regular basis about their child's progress, particularly about their education, health and social development. This will help to reduce the estrangement of the child from the family.

● There should be regular meetings between the carers, the parents and the child, held at times convenient for the family.

● Parents should be treated with respect at all times and regarded as partners not adversaries. Their visits should be valued and they should be encouraged to join in the routines of establishments, for example, meal times, planning of holidays, fundraising events, outings, school related activities, dental and medical examinations and shopping for their own children's clothes.

● Consideration needs to be given to the families' cultural, religious and linguistic needs. All residential staff should be aware of dietary rules, festivals, customs and dress regulations relating to the children in their care. Parents should always be consulted about personal grooming needs and hygiene.

● Children and young people must have access to a private telephone; supplies of writing paper, envelopes and stamps should be readily available on request.

● Private mail should not be withheld or opened. If a child has to be protected from threatening family members, staff should support the child to deal with an unwelcome letter.

● Parents should be encouraged to keep the establishment informed about changes in their circumstances or about significant family events which may have an impact upon the wellbeing of the child. This will work better if giving information is a two-way process.

● Parents should be invited to share in occasions which are of import-ance to the child, for example, birthdays, religious festivals, prize givings, sports days.

● It is often necessary to offer families help with transport arrangements or access to a building. Lifts to and from stations or bus stops can give a welcoming signal. A ramp can reassure people with disabilities that they are expected to visit their children.

● Residential staff also need support and should also be treated as partners by other professionals. Residential care should be seen as an integral part of any child and family service which must include contact.

Summary

Over 90 per cent of children in care return to live with a relative,[13] thus highlighting the importance of ensuring that family contact is main-tained. The proportion for whom contact would pose a serious risk of abuse or significant harm is small. From the research undertaken by the Dartington Research Unit, this group represented only four per cent of the sample.[14] Residential care, although primarily a service for children, needs also to be seen in the wider context of family support services. More consideration needs to be given to supporting families and to the balance between the power of the social worker and the rights and responsibilities of parents, particularly if a non-judgemental approach is to be adopted.

The Children Act 1989 places a clear obligation on care staff to 'endeavour to promote contact between children who are looked after by them and parents, people with parental responsibility, relatives, friends and persons connected with the child' (Sch 2, Para 15). The notion of partnership which underpins the Act contradicts the view that contact is likely to be damaging to, or in conflict with, the interests of the child or the work of children's homes. There is a clear need to promote contact for both profound psychological and emotional reasons, and for purely practical and more narrowly functional purposes. Research has shown that 'children in care are much more likely to have stable, more positive experiences when they maintain their links with their parents and wider family and friends, even if they are unlikely to return to live in their own home.'[15]

Whilst recognising the inevitable problems and irritations which will arise from being a partner in care, a co-pilot rather than captain, I would argue from experience that the potential gains for young people and parents, as well as for professional carers, are too important to allow contact to wither through failure on our part to do all we reasonably can to promote it.

References

1. Kelly G, *Natural parent contact – A theory in search of practice*, in *Permanent Substitute Families – Security or severance?*, Family Rights Group, 1984.

2. See 1 above.

3. See 1 above.

4. Jolly S C, 'Cutting the ties – The termination of contact in care', *Social Welfare and Family Law*, no 3. pp229–311, 1994.

5. Berridge D, and Cleaver H, *Foster Home Breakdown*, Blackwell, 1987.

6. Fox L, 'Two value positions in recent child care law and practice', *British Journal of Social Work*, no 12, pp 265, 1982.

7. Fanshel D, and Shinn E B, Social Services Inspectorate, *A Study of Local Authority Decision Making around Contact Applications under Section 34*, Department of Health, 1994.

8. Rowe J, and Lambert L, *Children who Wait*, Association of British Adoption Agencies, 1975.

9. Bullock R, Hosie K, Little M, Millham S, 'The problems of managing the family contacts of children in residential care', *British Journal of Social Work*, no 20, pp 591–610, 1990.

10. Berridge D, *Children's Homes*, Blackwells, 1985.

11. See 9 above.

12. Thorpe R, 'Consumers' viewpoint', *Social Work Today*, 4:3, 1974.

13. See 9 above.

14. Millham S, Bullock R, Hosie K, Haak M, *Lost in Care: The problems of maintaining links between children in care and their families*, Aldershot: Gower, 1986.

15. Sinclair R, *Residential Care and the Children Act 1989: A resource pack for staff in residential child care settings*, National Children's Bureau, 1991.

9   Contact and foster carers

Pat Verity

Pat Verity is the Policy and Services Manager of the National Foster Care Association.

'My home is where I live, bring up my family, yet it is also a foster home. It is both my private and my public life.'

The above could have been said by any foster carer trying to make sense of the openness of their home and the balancing act that carers have to perform to ensure that their family can continue to have a private life, that their fostered children can benefit from being with them, and that they retain their uniqueness as a foster family. There is an expectation that carers will welcome strangers into their homes with little or no information, allow them a great deal of freedom, and create a situation where parents and children can relax in each others company. However, social workers need to keep the difference between a foster home and a residential home at the front of their minds, when contact arrangements are being negotiated.

Why should contact be seen as difficult?
Contact with children's families is often seen as the most difficult part of fostering. For many carers this stems from the way that they have been recruited. They may have been approved at a time when the child was the main focus of recruitment campaigns, with little mention made of parents or other family members. They may have come forward for a specific child, prior to the changes in legislation which sought to encourage contact between children and their families. Workers may have glossed over the effect that having other people in their homes would have on the carers' family life, and not adequately prepared them for the reality. Inadequate preparation and training may have a strong impact on the way that foster carers actually deal with parents' visits.

Training material produced by the National Foster Care Association (NFCA) since the end of the 1970s has included the implications of working with parents and the wider family and the rewards that this can bring. In the video, *Choosing to Foster*,[1] a carer explains her approach to working with parents:

'I'm trying to get really good relationships with them and I make them comfortable. I talk to them and tell them "you're the child's mum or dad. It's just for me to care for them".'

However, the reality for many people can be very different from the theory – better or worse than expected.

Many foster families take more than one child at a time. Indeed, Berridge and Cleaver's book, *Foster Home Breakdown*,[2] positively reinforces the idea that it is better for a fostered child to be in a family where there are other fostered children. But each new child in the foster home brings with them other people who have responsibilities to and for them: their parents and wider family, their friends, and their social worker. The foster carers and their existing children will already have their own networks, and in many instances, a specialist fostering worker. This adds up to a large number of people and relationships. Any foster family starts from a base of wanting to retain the essential elements of family life – if these are destroyed then why should foster care be better than residential care for children? Carers must therefore seek to involve other people who are not directly part of the family, whilst ensuring that they can still operate as a family unit.

Making sure that contact arrangements are workable and agreeable must be a number one priority for the child's social worker. There is no point in making plans which stipulate the amount of contact that a family will have with their child, without first giving thought to how this can be achieved. If it is to be in the foster home, can the foster carers cope with the amount of contact that is being considered? Are the times convenient or will they clash with arrangements that the foster carers already have, either for their own child, this child, or for other fostered children?

Planned contact

The separation of the care plan for children from the foster placement agreement can create difficulties. Foster carers will usually be presented with plans which have been agreed with parents, without any opportunity to comment on them, to understand why they have been formulated, or to suggest alternatives. Social workers may then become frustrated with the carer and see them as obstructive, as not understanding the parent's or social worker's point of view.

There has to be a way this can be prevented.

Ideally, carers should be involved in the planning process and social workers should do their utmost to involve them; if this is not feasible, carers need to know that there will be some flexibility in the arrangements that are suggested, and to know the purpose of the contact: assessment, rehabilitation or continuity.

Another way forward is for all carers to work out what contact, in broad terms, they can agree to for any child. This obviously needs to be reconfirmed for each placement because the circumstances in the home may change from time to time. The maximum amount of contact the foster family will welcome should be recorded on their files, and this information taken into consideration before approaches are made to take a particular child.

> *'I sometimes wonder if it is better to have the coachload on Friday afternoon, rather than the small groups throughout the week.'*

This carer was describing her experience of children who rarely have only one person to whom they appear strongly attached. They may have parents, grandparents, past carers, and friends who will want to keep in touch. Carers often have the day-to-day task of identifying who is important to the child in relation to key issues and decisions, and who needs to be reassured that the child is safe and well. Laying down ground rules, like telephoning before visits, helps to ensure that relationships are not jeopardised because the carer is unable to cope with either the amount of contact, the number of people involved, or the sheer inconvenience of unheralded visits.

> *'Sometimes it just isn't convenient. I try my hardest not to refuse a parent who rings up and wants to come and see their child, but occasionally it does clash with something I am doing. For instance it was my daughter's school play and we were all going. Do we let her down, or do we say "No" to the parent?'*

Carers often remark that someone needs to explain to parents what fostering is, and who the people are who provide it, but they also feel that unless social workers understand the benefits and realities of placing a child in family care, then it will be little wonder that parents have unrealistic expectations.

The same could be said of the courts. Social workers have returned from courts to tell carers that a judge or magistrate has ordered that contact is to take place in the foster home, x times per week for x number of hours. These orders have been made without any consideration or consultation with the foster family. Solicitors and social workers must ensure that demands made by courts can be met and are realistic, otherwise carers who wish to refuse could be held in contempt of court.

There will be situations where the child/young person is refusing to have contact with their family. Carers will then need to consider the child/young person's ability to make decisions, and may have to support them in discussing their reasons with the social worker. However, a refusal to have contact should not be seen as the decision for all time. Relationships between children and their parents are constantly changing, and carers who are sensitive can work with both the young person and their parent toward a long-term goal.

Drawing up the Foster Placement Agreement should be the perfect opportunity for relatives, social worker and foster carers to discuss the advantages and disadvantages of foster placements and the practical arrangements needed to maximise the likely success of the placement. The agreement is the base from which future relationships can and will develop. If it leaves areas ill-defined, then confusion can result. A properly drawn up agreement that everyone "signs up to" can be used as a means of quality control and will ensure that there are appropriate methods for reviewing decisions as the situation develops.

The benefits of contact

As a carer, what are the potential benefits in keeping contact going? Many carers still feel that rescuing children from harmful parents is what fostering is all about. Whilst social workers will do their best to get them to change their views during assessment and training, this idea may linger. Some people find it very difficult indeed to put themselves in another person's shoes. As a result, the gap between the foster carer and the child's parent can be wide. Many foster carers lead very different lives from the parents of the children they look after. This may be because of differences in class, ethics or culture. Even where children are placed in foster families of the same racial and religious background, there can be enormous differences between families, and it is important that children do not get messages that their parents are not "good enough" because they are not encouraged to have contact. If foster carers can accept the child's parents then the child too will feel accepted.

> *'We started fostering when we were in our 20s. It was just after the 1960s and the mini skirt. This mum's mini skirt was more like a belt round her waist than a skirt. I really didn't want to be seen walking out with her yet I knew it was important that I involved her as much as possible with T's care, going to the clinic, etc. When I look back I wonder how I could have been such a prude – but I think that's because I'm much more confident now, as well as times having changed.'*

One of the major benefits of contact is that foster carers can begin to understand problems that parents face.

> *'When I saw the bare boards, the lack of furniture, realised that there was no hot water, and that this single mum had to lug a pram up the stairs because the landlord wouldn't let her keep it in the hall, I wondered how I'd have coped in those circumstances.'*

There are clear benefits for children if they can see their parents, family and friends. They know that being fostered does not mean they have been forgotten. It can bring reassurance to a child who feels that the bottom has dropped out of their world, if at least there is some continuity in their lives. Contact with their family enables children to know who they are in order to develop and grow. This is important whether the child is staying long term, returning home, or moving on to a new permanent family. Children who are going back home need to know that both their home and their family are there for them to go back to.

> *'When I look back at the children I've cared for where I've been party*

to decisions to stop contact I feel ashamed. Children have a right to their identity.'

There will be occasions when face to face contact with parents may not be appropriate but other relatives, particularly grandparents, may be the support that a child needs. Even if all face to face contact is impossible for some children, contact which promotes continuity through exchange of information is beneficial to everyone. Imagine what it is like not knowing what is happening in your child's or grandchild's life. Foster carers can help alleviate the frustration, pain and anger of parents and other relatives by ensuring that helpful information is passed on, either directly between the adults, or through the child's social worker. Information needs to be two-way and also given to children so that they can be reassured and helped to make sense of what has happened to them.

Keeping indirect contact going between children and parents is a skill carers develop in long-term fostering arrangements. A decision that a carer will be the person to give children or parents information may change as the child matures. A carer who might have handled all the phone calls when a child was young, but who encouraged the child to speak to their parents, or write simple letters, might move easily to a situation where the child/young person instigates contact.

'It's knowing when the time is right for the child, which doesn't necessarily coincide with when it feels right for us. Although, looking back, if we've made the effort to support the young person in their wishes it's worked well.'

For the parents, visits offer the obvious benefit of seeing where their children are living and who is looking after them. For foster carers this can be a time to share information and learn something about the way the children respond to their parents. At the beginning of a placement, parents talking about a child's reactions to certain situations, the sort of food they like, the words they use, will help the foster family and child enormously. It also gives the parent a sense of doing something valuable for their child.

'Because she listened to me and reassured me that she would

follow the routine I had, I felt happy about leaving my little one with her.'

This mother was reassured by the carer who was going to look after her 18 month old child. The carer involved her in the placement, and made it clear that she didn't want to usurp the parent's position, nor did she want to make life difficult for the mother, when the child returned home.

'I prefer it if I can meet the parent alone before a child is placed. Then we can size one another up and check out whether we can work together. I can work with any child, but if I can't work with the parent and vice versa, then I know it's going to be an uphill struggle.'

This very experienced carer has managed to help many parents regain control over their lives and their children.

'I believe parents can change and though they may have failed in the past it doesn't mean that this has to continue.'

She is always very clear with parents about the expectations their children will have of them, what is important and what is not. For instance, she emphasises the need for a good relationship between parent and child, and that parents will be judged on this, not on whether their home is beautifully clean and tidy. By working in this way with parents, she has enabled them to be reunited with their children when social workers had "given up on them".

A carer of teenagers has found that with encouragement, all the young people they have looked after have wanted their parents to meet them, and that this has been achieved within the first or second day.

'The young people invite them to meet us and then we arrange for their parents, if they want to, to have a meal with us.'

Another carer commented thus:

'It's easy for us to read into a child's reactions what we would like to believe and there are some social workers who collude with us. For instance, we have all seen children who have reacted angrily to a parent's visit, or have "blocked them out". We could take this to mean that the child does not want to see their parent and reinforce this with

the messages we give to their mum or dad. We have to learn to be honest with ourselves and really look at what is best for children and separate that from our own feelings'.

This carer was describing a very common dilemma. How the carer subsequently acts can have far-reaching consequences. If the carer implies to the parent that it would be a good idea to give the child time to settle down before visiting or contacting them again, then the parent will go away feeling guilty for having caused the child distress and may be reluctant to visit at all. When they do pluck up courage, the child is likely to react even more strongly. However, if the carer is able to assure the parent that the child's reaction is normal, and is one they would expect of their own child, and that it will get better, then the parent will go away encouraged.

Children have a right to continuity in their lives. If keeping them in touch with their families maintains continuity, then the child, the parents, and the carers will all benefit.

Welcoming families

Parents and other relatives can feel very vulnerable. Arriving at a foster home is difficult, particularly if they have not met the carers before. The way in which they are welcomed will make all the difference. A grandparent described having to visit her grand-daughter in someone else's home as the "most unbelievable feeling". She said:

'I'd have just liked these people to say yes, it was OK to visit, and to give me some encouragement like saying that my grand-daughter was looking forward to me coming. That would have helped me relax because it was a very tense situation. I would have really liked them to appreciate that I was her grandmother.'

The way in which carers first greet parents and other family members can set the tone for relationships which can go on for many years. The parent who was able to describe how grateful she had been to the carer for the way in which she was welcomed into the home, given a cup of coffee, and treated as if she were just another friend visiting, immediately felt at ease. The carer did nothing to suggest that the children had improved whilst they had been with her. She did, however, ask the parent's advice about how to deal with difficulties. The parent appreciated this, and was then able to say that the children had grown and were doing well.

Problems

Foster families need clear information which will prevent them causing distress to a child's family. Carers need to know what is not acceptable. Difficulties will of course be fewer if parents are involved in day-to-day decisions. A black parent talking about why placing his daughter with a black family was important said the following:

> 'Black children should grow up with black people. Black people see the children's skin more clearly than white people because we have different skin from white people. There is a lot that children need to know about our roots, our background. We do have a different approach to life.'

There are differences between all families – no two are alike. The differences may be greater when the foster family and the child's family do not share the same culture and religion or sexuality. This could mean that one or both of the families feel uncomfortable working with the other. One white parent commented on visiting his child's new foster family (the second set of carers to have looked after his child):

> 'I feel much happier here. The family are ordinary and down to earth like us. The others had airs and graces and you never felt relaxed.'

A carer explains:

> 'We always make sure that parents know that we are lesbians before they come to our home. As far as we can see they don't seem to have a problem with this but I think that's because we are open and honest with parents.'

Foster carer training must ensure that carers value other people who have very different life experiences to themselves.

Carers may resent parents questioning their children. For instance, asking simple questions such as 'Has Joyce taken you to the park?' can be seen as a criticism by a harassed carer, who might be feeling guilty that she hadn't had the time. If such an ordinary query is taken the wrong way, how much more can be read into 'Does Joyce smack you?' But even that might be an innocent enquiry from parents who believe in smacking their children.

'We know that if the boot were on the other foot, we would be questioning anyone who had care of our children, and would be asking our children questions in order to get at what we saw as the truth. It is difficult to accept this, though, when you are the person who is under scrutiny.'

Unlike social workers, carers cannot "go home" at the end of the day. Usually parents will know where they live, and so it is possible to make contact at any time of the day or night. Parents who have built up a good relationship with carers may do this in order to resolve their own problems, which are nothing to do with the child who is being fostered. There may be other parents who do not like the carers and are resentful of the fact that their child is being looked after. They may make a nuisance of themselves, ringing up or turning up on the doorstep on the "off chance", or when they have had too much alcohol. Many carers say that they can cope with the scenes – it's their neighbours who don't like it!

'After this particular evening when B's dad turned up drunk and was abusive outside the house, life was never quite the same with our neighbours. First they were aloof, and then the social services department started getting anonymous phone calls about our care of the children. We're sure it was one of our neighbours who thought we'd lowered the tone of the neighbourhood.'

Perhaps the assessment of carers needs to be extended to the neighbours. Some carers have gone out of their way to involve neighbours in their decision to foster. Others have become foster carers knowing that there will be opposition. Local authorities have to respond when there are anonymous allegations, but the level of belief has to be fairly measured against what is known of the carers and the circumstances in which they are operating.

Carers who have to cope with contact from all members of split families can be "piggy in the middle", with mum and her family on one side and dad on the other with his family. The carer is expected to balance the needs of all these people who are involved with the child, and not to make judgements which will be counter-productive. Because they will rarely have only one child in placement, these problems will be multiplied.

There are carers who have to take one child to a Family Centre because it has been considered unsafe to allow contact anywhere else, whilst another child they are looking after may have contact in the foster home. In situations like this, carers have to be sensitive to the messages given to children who may feel that their family is not good enough to come to the foster home. This could then affect their behaviour and cause additional stress to the foster family.

Many carers have to make complicated travel arrangements. Getting a child to and from a Family Centre, at the same time as trying to collect children from a number of schools, is difficult. It can raise carers' anxiety levels as they become concerned that delay at one destination may have a knock on effect on the other children.

'If only social workers would think about how the arrangements can be achieved, and recognise that they must take some responsibility for ensuring that they can be.'

Transporting children safely must be seen as a high priority for social workers and carers. Ad hoc arrangements with transport departments or local cab offices may not be the most appropriate. Some agencies have developed supportive networks around foster families which can be used for contact and other arrangements. For example, a single carer explained why she needed more help, and the agency now pays the relative of another carer (who has been assessed and checked) to provide assistance with transport and respite.

There are cases where carers do not agree with the social worker's plans for rehabilitation, but haven't been able to be honest about their feelings, or if they've expressed them, believe that they haven't been heard. Unless these feelings are recognised and dealt with, the rehabilitation plans can be unconsciously sabotaged by the carer. Honesty between the carers and social worker is paramount, even if they have widely differing views.

'I said that she'd be back in care in eighteen months if she went home and the social worker accepted my view. We all agreed it was right to try though.'

Only if problems are jointly addressed can an agreement be reached about the work to be undertaken.

'As far as I knew the baby had been burnt by the mother and I wasn't happy about her going back home. At the social worker's suggestion I took her back to her mother and I am glad I did because I could see that they were delighted to see each other – the burn was an accident, but this had never been communicated to me.'

Names, and in particular, what fostered children call their carers, can cause great problems if the children fall into the habit of calling them "mum" and "dad". A parent in the video, *Choosing to Foster,*[3] articulates parents' views clearly.

'I was very angry when they (SSD) had this silly notion that she had a foster "mother". She has one mother, and that's me.'

No parent wants to hear their child calling someone else "mum" or "dad", yet if they do, the child will possibly only be copying the other children in the home and will not have made a conscious decision to replace their own parents. This needs careful handling. The best course might be for carers to specify a name which any child in the household may use for them. If, however, they are generally called "mum" or "dad", then they need to explain and remind the fostered child to use a special name, and to talk frankly with the parent, so that they understand the lack of significance for the child if slips are made.

Many carers complain about parents who come loaded with presents for their children, but totally ignore the children of the foster family. Foster carers' families on the other hand, usually make sure they include the fostered child in any "treats". One carer described being brought down to earth by her young son, when she was heard complaining about the pile of presents which had yet again been loaded onto the fostered child. His reaction was, 'Well, she is all they've got, isn't she . . .' Out of the mouths of babes!

Contact with siblings

The importance of keeping brothers and sisters in touch may not be recognised either by social workers or foster carers who could have ambivalent feelings about their past relationship, or the additional work involved. Social workers may have difficulties in organising contact arrangements because they are likely to fall outside a normal working day. They might assume that the practical problems are too great to be overcome; for instance, the distance or the cost involved in maintaining contact.

Foster carers often feel that they have not been given sufficient information in order to reassure children about their brothers and sisters, and even when they know that other children from the family are also being looked after, they may not know where and with whom. This increases the likelihood that children will quickly lose contact with those who are important to them and research shows that it is siblings with whom they most want to retain contact.

Foster carers need to be given permission to maintain contact with brothers and sisters of their fostered children. There are examples of good working arrangements where foster families who are unable to take large sibling groups work closely with another family nearby, to ensure that the children can have as much contact as possible; they organise after school meetings, joint outings, and visits to the park. Whilst it may not be feasible to provide sleeping accommodation for large groups of children, most foster families can find the space for them to play and share time together, and it can help to spread the burden if each of the families takes a turn. In this way, a picture of the sibling relationships can be built up which would be impossible if the only time they met was for one hour a week. Some foster families have gone further and decided, in discussion with the children's social worker, that they can offer a weekend visit, often in less than ideal sleeping conditions, to achieve an even better assessment. However, such invitations should be approached with caution. If there has previously been an abusive relationship between the children, carers need to have full information so that they do not create situations which would encourage or facilitate further abuse. They need to know about all the children they will be involved with, even those living elsewhere, so that they can assist them to understand the reasons for separation and help them to continue appropriate relationships.

Clarity, openness and responsibility

Carers should never be unclear about their role in contact arrangements. Are they there just to facilitate the visit in a friendly environment? To act as a supervisor, assessor, or to provide some training for a parent? The parents also need to know. Carers who have not been given full information, or who are uncertain about their position, may fail to protect a previously abused child. That child may then feel betrayed by the foster family. Or the fostered child may have been the instigator of abuse and may resent the carer's watchful eye. Describing the task required of carers, and being honest with everyone about it, can prevent misunderstandings and difficult situations.

Parents come into foster homes knowing that carers have been assessed as capable of looking after their children. It puts them at a disadvantage, because they have been judged not to be capable, for whatever reason. It is understandable that they may want to criticise the care being given, so they can say "we were not that bad after all". Carers and parents together need to accept that there will be difficulties in their relationships, but that everyone is working for the same end – the best for the child. It is vital for carers to believe that the needs of the majority of children can be best met by their parents in order to work successfully with families.

Often carers will be expected to act as unpaid social workers by parents. Many parents believe carers are halfway between being an "ordinary" person and a social worker. As a result they will tell carers things that they don't feel confident enough to tell the social worker. Sometimes, they will do this wanting the carer to pass the information on, and at other times, wanting the carer to help them reach a decision about what to do. Carers need to be honest with parents; their responsibility as a foster family is to act in the best interests of children. There will be occasions when a carer will become concerned during a contact visit by something a parent has either said or done. Parents need to know that a carer must share this information with the social worker. How this is done is crucial.

'I always make a point of going over any concerns with a parent so they know what I'll be saying. I also show them anything that I record about visits, contact, etc'.

This carer has developed an open style with parents, which they usually appreciate. They don't walk into situations where they have no idea what is going to be said about them. This carer is also able to help parents recognise how well they are doing because she, like many others, keeps a clear record of contact visits, the time spent by the parent with the child, and what takes place. Such information can be invaluable to agencies who are trying to make decisions about the child's future; there is a difficulty for carers who do not want to be seen as "spies" by parents, yet the information could be essential in helping to reunite a family.

Carers can feel very confused about plans for children. Frequently they will see the positive side of parents and will question why a child should not be living at home. Social workers who are open to hearing others' views, and valuing them, can work with carers to change course.

Court proceedings
A major issue in relation to contact is that carers could be helping to collect evidence for court proceedings. This is more common in short-term fostering, but can also apply in long-term placements.

Carers need to have continuing working relationship with parents, even after making statements about a parent and child which result in a court order. Social workers do this all the time. They may face aggression from a parent for a while, but they can go home. Carers can't. Parents eventually come to terms with the fact that the social workers were only doing their job; but it is far harder for them to reach this understanding in relation to carers. And carers do not have the same protection. Their home is vulnerable and all they can rely on is their ability to calm a parent based upon the relationship they have developed.

After an unwelcome court order, carers often become a target and can find themselves getting the abuse from parents that would be reserved for social workers in other circumstances.

'The parent we were working with lived nearby. We had tried hard to get her involved with her child, but for some reason she didn't respond. She had a lot of anger against the social worker, but seemed to be able to hold this in check. However, every time she saw us in the street we would get the whole lot thrown at us – when she did actually come to our home she was fine, but I suppose what she needed to do was put on a display for the other people on our housing estate.'

This carer also talked about the troubles that follow, even when a child is no longer living with them.

'Because J lived locally we still continue to see his mum even though J has been adopted by another family. She finds it very difficult when she sees us and so we are often verbally abused in the street.'

A parent who verbally abuses a carer is awkward to handle. A parent who physically attacks a carer and their property is even worse. Understandably, carers feel angry if they discover that a particular parent is known to be violent but they haven't been told of this, or a social worker has failed to provide support. Carers tell stories of social workers who are not even willing to be present on visits or to tackle parents about their behaviour. This leaves foster families feeling threatened and isolated, often resulting in a child having to leave an otherwise satisfactory placement.

Agencies need to have clear policies about the support that will be provided during, for example, supervised visits, and in the worst case, following court injunctions.

Foster carers who feel confident that they will have the backing of their agency might be able to prevent problems arising by talking authoritatively to parents, so preventing the escalation of a conflict.

After a placement ends

If a child has been returned home and the carers supported the decision, then they can often continue to play a key role, but for some this is not so:

'It's like he is dead.'

'We've not been given any information about him.'

These are typical comments from carers who, having looked after a child for quite a lengthy period, were then expected by social workers and/or the child's parents, to have no further interest in the child. They describe the feelings as akin to a bereavement and in many ways experience the same sense of loss that parents have described.

'Why, when we are taught that it is better for children to have continuing contact with their parents to ensure continuity, are we then expected to totally disappear from their lives when children move on from us?'

This is a fair question from carers. Ideally, children need continuity from their ex-carers, as well as from their parents and wider family, but this may be hard if a parent wants to make a clean break with the past. Foster carers should at least be given information by social workers who nearly always continue to work with a family; and children should be told that their ex-carers ask about them, even if they do not see them.

When children are returned home, social workers may feel that they have no control over what a parent does about keeping a child in touch with previous carers. They can, however, make sure that they tell parents about the benefits of contact – much easier of course, if the parents have felt welcomed by the carers when their child was being looked after!

If a child is placed with adopters or other foster carers, the local authority social worker has much more power and say in arrangements. They can ensure that contact does take place, at least until such time as an adoption order is made. A good relationship with a carer does not prevent a child from making a good relationship with a new substitute parent – in fact the opposite is true. The evidence that the child can make attachments could encourage the new parents at a time when they might be feeling quite down, possibly because the child is not being very responsive. The carer can also provide support to an adoptive family if allowed to. No foster carer should be in a position to present a threat to an adopter, but equally, foster families should not feel so pushed out that their only way of continuing contact is by seeking legal redress.

The costs
Keeping contact between children and their families alive and healthy,

is expensive. The true costs are rarely considered when placements are made, and there is an assumption that the fostering rate will be sufficient and that carers will manage it all! It is impossible not to provide a parent, or other relatives, with a meal if they are in the foster home at a time when the family is going to eat. Taking children back to their own homes for visits, or visiting brothers and sisters in other foster or adoptive homes costs money. Keeping children in touch with their friends can be expensive, particularly if the children are not old enough to travel by themselves. The telephone bill in a foster home is likely to be significantly higher than for a similar non-foster family. Even local phone calls can soon produce a sizeable bill. How much greater will it be if the parent lives at the other end of the country, or even abroad?

Parents too, will have costs which should not be forgotten by carers and social workers. Income support payments do not go far when trying to keep in touch with children.

Dealing with abuse

Probably the most difficult situation for both carers and parents is when there is contact and one of the parties is alleged to have abused the child. Whilst most people can acknowledge that there might be the faint possibility that anyone could strike a child when they were out of control, there is no sympathy for people who sexually, or systematically physically abuse children. Both bring out strong feelings, although sexual abuse, because it crosses all the generational and social boundaries, elicits the strongest aversion.

Foster carers should not be left alone to handle charged situations with alleged perpetrators of children they are looking after.

'I could never forgive the social worker . . . he knew that the child was scared of her father but ignored what was going on in my sitting room.'

Foster families need precise, written guidance when dealing with contact with alleged perpetrators. It is helpful to discuss with an expert, together with the social worker, how the visits should be handled, and what to do when there are concerns.

Whilst foster carers are prepared for their feelings towards alleged perpetrators during training sessions, it is unlikely that they will have had training to deal with the possibility that they, the carers, are thought to have abused a child.

> '*Continuing to work with the family after what they'd said, even though the department investigated and exonerated us, was more stressful than dealing with the allegation itself.*'

In time, some carers have found that they have been able to use such painful experiences to learn about themselves and become more compassionate towards parents. However, it is not a route to be recommended, and steps can be taken to reduce the likelihood of an accusation being made.[4]

Social work support

Carers need social workers to support them. They need workers who can accept that there will be problems and who will assist in resolving them. For instance, social workers need to talk to children honestly about why particular arrangements are made for them.

All carers need to know the purpose of contact for each child in their care and they need as much information as possible about the timing of contact arrangements and how they are to be financed, as well as the procedures for changing them.

Family placement workers are central in acting as brokers in contact arrangements. As more and more local authorities turn social workers into case managers, it is predictable that they will be seeking the perfect service for their client. Neither foster care nor residential care is a perfect service. Both are unnatural situations for children, and any placements that are made have to take this into account and not seek to produce an ideal solution. Family placement workers have the fostering expertise and will have knowledge of the expectations which have already been placed on the carers by different social workers and parents. Without the expertise of workers closely involved in fostering when contact arrangements are made, and a recognition of the reasons why foster care is the preferred option, foster families will be set up to fail. They will be seen as the people who have been obstructive rather than helpful. Social workers have responsibilities to negotiate contact which is workable, and to encourage parents to value foster care for their children and to accept their own part in making contact work.

Conclusion

Contact is a challenging aspect of working with families. Many foster carers have developed skills in this area through their work with a variety of families. Through contact, they frequently see a side of parents that "official" staff don't see. Their skills need to be appreciated and expanded, so that foster carers are valued as members of the fostering team. The strength of foster care is that it is a personal service to children and families. It is based on a belief that families (including single adults) can offer the best care for children. Giving foster carers a proper status in the agency, and defining the part that foster carers play in promoting contact with parents, will increase the professional credibility of the service.

It is useful to remind ourselves that when contact works well, it can change people's lives.

'When I started having Nadine stay overnight with me her foster carer wrote out a rota for me telling me what time Nadine goes to bed, gets up, what she likes to eat. Some of it I knew, but it was really helpful to have. What I really appreciated was that she rang me in the evening and in the morning to give me encouragement. She was so pleased for me. She still phones and comes to see me and Nadine.'

References

1. *Choosing to Foster*, NFCA, 1994.

2. Berridge D, and Cleaver H, *Foster Home Breakdown*, Blackwell, 1987.

3. See 1 above.

4. *Safe Caring*, NFCA, forthcoming publication.

10 A care leaver's perspective of care and contact

Zena Dickson

Zena Dickson was previously in care.

When considering this title, I thought about what the word "contact" meant to me as a young person in care. It meant an opportunity to see the ones I loved, to exchange emotions and feelings, and to share memories. There are different types of contact but whatever form it takes, to me it means the same as communication, as contact cannot take place without it.

The New Oxford Dictionary defines "contact" as a 'condition or state of touching, meeting or communicating.' Communication or contact may be written, verbal or non-verbal. Not only is contact necessary between a young person and their family, but it is also imperative that there be solid and regular interaction between social workers and young people. In my opinion the word "contact" ought to be used in its broader sense to include telephone calls, personal visits, sending letters, pictures or cards and physical contact. As part of my research and for the purposes of this chapter, I have interviewed some young people who are currently in care or accommodated. As far as they are concerned, there is no difference in how it feels. When I use the term "in care" I refer to all children who are looked after by local authorities, I have included their contributions in an attempt to illustrate some of the points I will be making.

Being in care

The experience of being in care can be difficult to overcome. Dealing with the pain and frustration is a complicated and troublesome task. For many young people the emotional stress is overwhelming. No one really chooses to be in care. Some young people may insist that they "want" to go into care but I am sure that, given the choice, they would rather change the situation at home and stay there. Being uprooted from your family can have long-term effects on your self-image and self-esteem.

Negative feelings can take over and leave you feeling insecure and vulnerable. This ultimately influences the way you live your life as a young adult.

Coming to terms with separation and/or rejection can take many years. When in care, it is as though you have become lost in the system; simply passed from pillar to post. You feel like a number or even an object that has no right to have feelings or emotions. At times you feel as though you are just a burden on society. The institutional structures are frustrating and can distance you from reality. You often wonder if anyone is concerned about you, if anyone cares about how you feel. No one seems truly to understand you and this results in you feeling so alone. The lonely empty feeling seems to grow rapidly while at the same time your confidence in adults declines. Nothing in your life seems private; someone somewhere has documented and mapped out your future. They have categorised and branded you according to their own stereotypes. This is distressing and confusing as you feel as if you have no control over what is occurring in your life. The sadness and loneliness deepen when social workers and foster carers discourage contact and sometimes even alienate you from your parents. What they feel is protecting you can, in fact, be promoting and enhancing the long-term emotional trauma young people in care experience. Although circumstances differ for each young person, I am sure many will be able to relate to these feelings.

The time a young person spends in care should not be only to protect them, but to help them rebuild their lives and to deal with and overcome any difficulties that they may have experienced at home. It should also be to restore the young person to a satisfactory level of competence, and to give them the same or similar opportunity as their counterparts who were not in care. It appears to me that the overcoming and restoring part in this scenario has become lost within the institutional structures of social service departments.

Care leavers are failing to overcome the difficulties that they have experienced in care. This is in part due to the lack of support given to young people. Research[1,2,3] now shows that care leavers are over-represented amongst the homeless. Although only about one per cent of the under 18 population are in care at any one time, some shocking

25–40 per cent of homeless people under the age of 21 are young people who have been in care. Educational achievements for care leavers are lower than that of the general population. Between April and September 1993, Centrepoint saw 199 care leavers, of whom 46 per cent had no formal qualifications and 44 per cent had no income whatsoever and were experiencing severe poverty and deprivation. It comes as no surprise that other studies found that only 13 per cent of care leavers managed to obtain full time employment within 3–9 months of leaving care. Furthermore, two and a half years after leaving care, 80 per cent were unemployed.

This lack of success and under-achievement will not change within the current structures of the care system. Social services and foster carers need to actively promote and encourage young people to rebuild and maintain family ties. They need to provide support to young people in their efforts to set up independently, but also to ensure that key family members are the base of the young person's support network. Parents can be a great source of support, even though they may have been inadequate in providing full-time care for the young person. One young woman said 'I know my mum has never really been a mother to me, yet despite this I just cannot stop loving her; not seeing her means that there is a gap in my life that cannot be filled.' Another said 'It does not matter how old you are, you always need your parents. I don't really class my mum as a mother, she's more of a friend.'

Some young people may say that they do not want to see their family. They may feel that they were rejected by their parents; it may not be easy for the young person to accept or admit that they feel love for their parents and family. It is as though accepting that you do love them is accepting the rejection. By accepting the rejection you have to accept and deal with the pain that goes with it. One young person said of her mother, 'My mum does feel guilty but I don't think that she realises the pain I feel because of her rejecting me.' Life can be difficult without the support of a family. Keeping in contact will give both the young person and their parents the opportunity to talk; to discuss things that may have gone wrong and to explain the way things have turned out. The word "sorry" if said with deep sincerity can heal the deepest of wounds. Another young person said, 'Now that I can't see my parents I really miss them.' She later went on to say, 'Sometimes I wish that I could see my parents, as it would make the world of difference to me. I suppose you don't know what you are missing till it has gone, and then sometimes it's too late.'

Dealing with contact

Contact is not only important if the young person is returning home, it is just as important when there are no apparent plans for the young person to return to their family. Arrangements for contact should be made as part of the plans for the child coming into care. After separation from their family, a young person needs constant reassurance that it was not their fault that the breakdown occurred, and that they are still loved. The feeling of being loved and being accepted is very reassuring. This is the opposite side of the coin to the cold feeling of isolation and loneliness. Young people can feel quite devalued when social workers or foster carers criticise their parents; saying that their parents are unfit carers and denying them the right to see their loved ones. Although many behavioural problems can stem from a low self-image and self-esteem, a young person may also be distressed after visits or contact with their parents and behave unpredictably as a result. This could be due to the emotional effect of the separation rather than the contact. The young person may then pick up any unease that is displayed by the foster carers, or see that the foster carers are visibly anxious. This may well make them feel that their birth family is under attack, and subsequently lead to a breakdown in the placement.

It may be difficult to cope with the competitiveness of having two families. Social workers and foster carers need to make allowances for this. It should be discussed so that the young person can make the relevant distinctions and deal with the situation in a way that is comfortable for them.

As a child you take the lead from your parents, and without them you can feel quite lost. When talking about what parents and families are, and what expectations young people have of them, there was quite a difference in opinion. One young person aptly said, 'Parents are supposed to look out for you, to care for you. They provide unconditional love; that's what families do.'

Aims and purpose of contact

The aims and purpose of contact can vary according to individual circumstances. The reason for contact can be just to keep the young person connected with their birth parents and other significant members of their family. By keeping connected, the young person will feel that they are a part of something larger, rather than being isolated. This will ultimately help with interpersonal, communication and social skills. It will also develop long-standing support networks for the young person when they leave care. Contact with families will give young people the opportunity to share memories and information about their past and background. Sharing memories does not mean sharing the *same* memories, people can remember different things about the same event.

Preparing for contact

Preparation for contact and visits is imperative, especially if time has elapsed. Social workers need to discuss with the young person what arrangements have been made, with full involvement from the beginning. Other important areas that need to be looked at are what the young person expects from having contact, and what they hope to achieve by it. Equally, what their parents hope to achieve should be communicated to them. Possibly a few pointers or guidelines could be given to both the young person and their parents on how to deal with difficult and frustrating situations. Social workers should be able to recognise and accept that the needs of the young person may differ from the needs of their parents. Both demands should be taken into account and some form of negotiation may have to take place. In cases where contact is supervised, gradually building privacy into the visit is crucial for older children, so that friendship and trust can develop. This does not have to be for long periods at a time; perhaps leaving them while the foster carer or social worker makes tea will enable just a small amount of privacy. Contact can feel artificial if no real exchange of emotions has taken place. If possible, parents should become involved in the day-to-day care of their children. Foster carers could invite them to dinner or for a family outing. Parents could perhaps offer overnight or weekend respite to the foster carers. Then the parents would not feel completely cut out.

Maintaining flexibility

Social workers, foster carers and parents need to be flexible and patient with young people. When a young person says that they do not want to see their parents, the door or opportunity for contact should always be left open. It should not be seen as a sign of instability if a young person continually changes their mind about whom they do and do not want to see. Rather, they should be encouraged to resolve any differences, and to build friendships within their family. If the young person does not currently want any face to face contact, I would strongly recommend that other forms of contact be sought. The key word is encouragement; social workers need to change the way they communicate with young people. They need to stop being reactive and become more proactive by encouraging regular contact. Even if the young person only agrees to accepting a letter or phone call from their parents, it is the beginning of a possible relationship. However, parents need to be made aware of the disappointment and pain the young person may feel if they do not turn up for arranged visits.

If the young person and their parents seem to be getting along particularly well, this should not immediately be interpreted to mean that the parents are now capable of providing proper care. In the past and speaking for myself, I was afraid to tell my social worker if my parental links were strengthening because of the fear of being sent back to an abusive home.

Although my relationship with my parents has been incredibly scarce and volatile, I have had extensive contact with members of my extended family. I cannot over-emphasise the immeasurable benefit that this has given me. Keeping in touch, maintaining and reviving those all important family bonds has enabled me to develop a positive image of myself.

Developing a strong identity

Being looked after by a local authority is clearly a disadvantage, and being black adds to your disadvantaged status. However, being black and in care but not having any sense of your culture or identity, and not knowing where you belong can make the overall situation even more difficult to overcome. Family ties are crucial, especially when the racial, cultural, religious or linguistic needs of the young person have not been successfully addressed during their time in care. There is no price for something as important or as valuable as preserving someone's culture and heritage.

After spending the first part of my life in a predominantly white environment, being placed with a black family was the most significant move for me. Before this I was confused about who I was and not at all confident about my culture. Through regular contact with key members of my family, I then leaned truly to value my heritage. Knowing who you are and where you come from is very important because without it you cannot plan for the future. Black children must be able to develop a personal identity and positive views of themselves and other black people, so that they can take pride in their heritage and resist having it devalued.

The need for consistency

There is a need for consistency in a young person's life. Continual changes of social workers do not help the young person to gain confidence in the system, especially when they are the last person to be told that their social worker is leaving, if they are told at all. Social workers ought to be more than just an acquaintance; they ought to build friendships, and not just visit in a crisis or to discuss arrangements for the next placement. Social workers should ensure that plans are made and reviews are on time and that the young person and their parents can be present. The young person should be told what their options are, and not just the ones that the department can afford or has available at the moment. Although lack of communication and information is one of the main causes for placement breakdowns, inappropriate placements made by social services is another. I have heard many horror stories of young people who have been lost in the system, having no reviews for a number of years and no contact with their social workers. This standard of care is not acceptable as these are real people being affected, not case studies from a text book. Social services departments must forge better links with the family, foster carers, and the community at large, so that no young person in care will be forgotten.

Family support

If we take a closer look at societies and cultures other than the British one, we will see that they make much better use of the extended family. Maybe we should learn from them and make use of other family members rather than alienate the young person from their family by putting them into care. Social services departments should be prepared to help the extended family financially. Although when family members show an interest in the well being of a young person, it should not be assumed that they want to take up full responsibility for them. No pressure should be put upon supportive family members as this may make any support dissolve and affect the young person in care who will continue to need the support of their family. I would go as far as to say that because leaving care is such an awful experience, it should not be done without the support of a family. In cases where contact has not been maintained, for whatever reason, social services departments ought to allocate a "contact worker" to these young people. They could do this by making use of their current foster care resources. They could use role models to provide support and encourage young people to become successful, to advise, befriend and assist them; to listen to them and help with any problems they may have; a mentor almost. Social services departments need to recognise the valuable work and time that some foster families can offer to care leavers.

Caring for young people

The current system is failing young people. It is as though the structures were set up to ensure that young people leave care as failures. It seems unrealistic to call them "social services" . . . I often wonder for whom they are providing a social service. Many young people in care feel that they have lost their families and have to fend for themselves because social services do not take proper responsibility for them.

The issue about young people having the right to decide is a sensitive area for me. I cannot see how a young person can objectively decide what is right for her, when she does not know all the options nor fully understands the long-term consequences of her actions. Social workers should not assume that because young people choose a particular course, that they accept the likely repercussions. Yes, young people do have the right to decide, but this should be within reason. If a young person was going to cause physical damage to himself, he would be prevented from doing so. Likewise, if he was going to do something that would affect his chances of equality and his long-term lifestyle, he should be advised and encouraged to change his mind. If young people refuse to go to school, then other forms of education must be discussed with them. Social workers should find out what they do not like about school and assess the way they are being educated. Discrimination at school may be the cause of educational failure and poor attendance. Without an education, it is difficult for young people to change their situation. Their suffering continues throughout their adult life, if they cannot compete in the job market. Education is not a choice, it is a necessity. According to the Children Act 'the welfare of the child should be paramount.' In my opinion, the welfare of the child includes the opportunity to achieve academically. There must be some boundaries set around the kind of choices given to young people and what they are capable of deciding; remembering that a child can only act as such and that they should be advised by family members who have parental responsibility.

Young people need to be encouraged and given recognition for achievements. Parents want you to achieve and to be successful. They will often go out of their way for you to succeed, particularly if this concerns your education or chosen career. In many families, parents will promise gifts to their children if they do well at school as a way of encouraging or pushing them to achieve. They may promise to pay for driving lessons if you pass your exams or even buy you a car. Maybe something similar could be adopted for young people in care which could also involve their parents. Possibly a tier system of pocket money whereby those who are in school get a higher amount. A system that would give recognition for qualifications and achievements based on individual ability. The leaving care grant could be based on the young person's performance. Something like this is needed to help families to encourage young people in care to push themselves, so that they too can achieve. But special attention needs to be paid to young people whose family bonds are irretrievably broken down. The young person's success cannot be left to chance, as it has been in the past. Contact with someone who will take a special interest in education and progress is required.

This may be a teacher, a social worker or a foster carer; it will have to be someone who can do what good parents should.

Addressing young people's needs

What structural changes are required to address the needs of young people? I am unable to give all the answers. I am sure though, that if social services change their approach to young people, particularly around the issues of contact, education and leaving care, then some improvements will be seen. It appears to me that there are many people who make money out of the misfortune of young people. I am well aware of the costs involved in keeping a young person in care and this seems such a waste. Especially if after their care experience young people are incapable of offering something to society. I cannot see how "80 per cent unemployment" among care leavers could possibly be a good reference for the current system. It is important that this imbalance is addressed. Admittedly, this will initially benefit young people who are separated from their families, but it will also be of benefit to society. Care leavers could be more effective members of the community and not have to rely on the government for a source of income.

If a child or young person who has been in care is placed back with their family, social workers should not presume that their services are no longer needed, nor that their work is complete. This is the start of a new phase for the young person and he or she needs help to settle and to become fully integrated with their family. Good communication with young people and their parents is a necessity. Even if the situation appears to have improved, it is important that the young person knows whom to contact if necessary. Social workers must remember that these families are fragile and vulnerable; they need to be handled with care. Consideration may have to be given to the needs of the young person over and above the needs of the family; reliable contact with social workers can make young people feel more secure when they return home.

Normally for young people, leaving home is a gradual process. They do not feel totally cut off, but rather they are made aware that there is always someone and somewhere to return to. Young people who leave care are thrown in at the deep end, without a life jacket, and with no guard to rescue them. It is impossible to envisage survival; no wonder so many of us drown. It is not only my wish, but the wish of many young people, that local authorities take their temporary role as "parents" more seriously.

Social workers should actively promote contact between young people and their permanent parents, siblings, extended family and family friends, so that children are not cut off from their roots. I propose that a young person's time in care could then be a positive and character building experience. Young people should be offered the opportunity to develop to their full potential and be prepared for the transition from childhood to adulthood. This transition should be a gradual process of independent living, supported by strong family links. This may mean more work, and more resources, but it will ultimately mean that the young people who have been looked after by local authorities can become integrated members of the community.

Finally, I would like to thank all the young people whom I interviewed for their valuable contributions. I hope that workers involved in the care of young people, will listen to these experiences and make the necessary changes to improve the services available for future generations.

References

1. *Out of Care and On the Streets*, Centrepoint, 1994.

2. Bichal N, Claydon J, Stein M, and Wade T, *Prepared for Living? A survey of young people leaving the care of three local authorities*, National Children's Bureau, 1992.

3. Stein M, and Carey K, *Leaving Care*, Blackwell, 1986.

11 The professionalisation of contact

Kate Morris

Kate Morris is a Social Work Adviser with the Family Rights Group.

The Children Act 1989, with its unprecedented relationship to research, gave legal and procedural importance to maintaining a child's connection with his or her family. In this chapter I suggest that in practice, contact arrangements are too often undertaken merely as an administrative and bureaucratic exercise. Consideration will here be given to family experiences and an alternative model of planning – Family Group Conferences – is described.

Current contact arrangements: family experiences
The Children Act acknowledges the need of almost all children to maintain links with their family network. The Act and its accompanying guidance and regulations makes clear the duties placed on local authorities to **promote** contact. A small but growing body of literature has begun to consider how best to meet these contact requirements.[1] Messages about good practice highlight the importance of contact in achieving effective outcomes for children,[2] and recent guides to planning for children place contact firmly on the agenda.[3] It can be argued that such developments are uniformly good for children and their families. However, evidence from family members is not always positive.

In a recent study of families' experiences of court processes following the implementation of the Children Act,[4] contact arrangements were often identified as difficult and negative. Some of the issues raised are listed below and illustrated with quotes from families.

Supervision of contact
   'My son came with two social workers who sat either side of him on the sofa. They were keeping control, this was not a natural situation.'

163

'I wasn't allowed to see him at Christmas or New Year because no-one was available to supervise. I proposed my home-start worker but social services refused . . .'

The venue

'Whenever we go to Mrs C's (the foster carer) we feel out of place . . .'

'The foster carers were always chopping and changing contact to suit themselves . . . social services were always more sympathetic to the foster carers' needs than ours because they were a family and we weren't and also because they were employed by social services.'

'The social worker decided where contact would take place. There was never any discussion about it being at home.'

The travelling

'The main problem was that he was in E, and it was too far to travel. We only used to go twice a week because of the journey and now they are saying I don't care about my son because I didn't go as often as I could.'

The cost

'I am not calling her as much now as I cannot afford it. I have to put £1 coins in because it is a long distance and you cannot do this on income support.'

'It is so artificial when you are out with children for four hours on a Saturday. You are not allowed to take them home and so you are hanging around in town. The children are always asking to go and do things or buy things which cost money and you have to keep saying no. You have no money to do anything with them when you are out . . . I feel this is very unfair.'

The contact between siblings

'The whole family has been blown to pieces and they are doing

nothing to maintain contact between the girls and their brother and sister . . .'

'The children only met up once a week for one hour during my contact visit. This made rehabilitation very difficult when they did come home because they had to get used to living together again. It was dreadful for the children to be separated.'

As these quotes illustrate, contact arrangements can be a source of frustration and distress. What quotes such as these also highlight is the local authority interpretation of the duty to "promote" contact as a duty to "organise" contact. Professionals can be argued to have assumed almost all the responsibilities associated with detailed arrangements for contact. Venues, timing, activities are all perceived to be decisions best made by professionals on behalf of children and their families. Yet, as the family study suggests, there is evidence that professionals would have to struggle to be any more than basic organisers of contact arrangements, having little time or energy to engage in quality considerations.

Such a bureaucratic approach to contact is time-consuming for professionals. Contact plans become vulnerable as other, seemingly more urgent, demands arise. Families describe with frustration the cancellation of contact because a worker is called away:

'Social services cancelled on a couple of occasions. I asked them to make the time up, but they wouldn't.'

Not only does the professional "ownership" of contact arrangements cause difficulties when juggling competing demands, it also generates significant problems in creating plans that accurately reflect a child's and family's circumstances.

'I'd run off and see my daughter for two hours and then race back home whilst the family aide brought my son here. I also had to attend various meetings with social services. There was no consideration as to whether this was convenient for me.'

In family life, who sees who, where and when can be a constantly changing pattern. Arrangements will reflect the particular traditions, culture and history of the family network. By deciding to organise contact arrangements professionals create a "service" which is delivered to family members. Such a service will inevitably reflect the resources available to the professional. Hence contact arrangements fail to reflect the diversity of need. Instead resource-led plans are generated, and factors such as venues, transport and supervision begin to determine the nature and the quality of the time children spend with their family members.

Family Group Conferences

Family Group Conferences originated in New Zealand. They were developed as a means of providing a respectful and accessible service to Maori families. The model was introduced in the UK some four years ago. Following developmental work undertaken by Family Rights Group, there are now approximately 20–25 local authorities and voluntary agencies either using or planning to use Family Group Conferences.[5]

The model sees the child's family network as the primary planning group. The basic process is as follows:

Referrals

The need for a Family Group Conference is agreed by the family and the professionals, and a co-ordinator is appointed. (Each local area will have its own criteria and processes for this.) The co-ordinator should reflect the race and culture of the family and share the same first language. All discussions are held in the family's language with, where necessary, the professionals using interpreters.

Stage I

The co-ordinator, in consultation with the child and his or her immediate family, identifies the family network. The term "family" is widely interpreted and includes relatives, friends and others significant to the child.

When inviting and preparing family members a date, time and venue for the meeting that are convenient for the family are agreed. (The co-ordinator has the right to exclude individuals if absolutely necessary.)

Stage II

At the start of the meeting the professionals explain to the family what their information is, any concerns that they may have, their statutory duties, and the relevant resources available. (Only those professionals directly involved, or holding significant information, should attend.) The family can clarify the information and ask any questions they might have.

Stage III

The co-ordinator and professionals withdraw, leaving the family to plan in private. The family has three basic tasks:

- to agree a plan;
- to agree contingency plans; and
- to agree how to review the plan.

The co-ordinator must be available during this time in case the family requires any help or additional information.

Stage IV

Once a plan is made, the co-ordinator and the key professionals meet again with the family, agree the plan and negotiate resources. The only reason for not agreeing the plan is risk of significant harm to the child. Contingency plans and reviewing arrangements are also agreed.

A Family Group Conference is not a "one-off" meeting. It is a process, and experience indicates the importance of families feeling able to hold several meetings if necessary.

Many practitioners have responded enthusiastically to the model, and see it as a meaningful way of achieving partnership.[6] A current study by Family Rights Group, as yet unpublished, identifies very positive responses from family members. Participants feel their views and suggestions have a real part to play in achieving an effective plan.

The model can generate professional anxieties. In particular, staff struggle with the powerful and responsible role the model gives to families. Family Group Conferences are based on a strength model. Families are seen as having a positive contribution to make when planning for children, even if some family members are experiencing or causing difficulties. By using this model, plans can be generated which accurately reflect and respect a child's race and culture and also explore the often hidden resources held by the extended family.

The model is not a "cheap option". Whilst relatives and others may offer help in a wide variety of ways, practical and financial assistance is often needed to allow the family's plans to work. Experience to date shows families create realistic, effective plans that meet children's needs in a way professional plans cannot. Family plans have used relatives as befrienders, agreed protective action, placed children within their network, pulled together significant adults to help achieve successful return home, and identified contingency plans for carers experiencing difficulties. Children have talked positively of the plans; they have felt pleased people came to "their" meeting, and they have commented that the plans produced are far more appropriate than those proposed by professionals.

Family Group Conferences and contact

Family Group Conferences are being used across almost all aspects of child care planning, and contact is an obvious area in which to develop their use.

Some Family Group Conference projects are already paying particular attention to contact issues. Specifically, Family Group Conferences are being used to help develop and maintain contact arrangements for care leavers, and to consider contact plans when a child is being placed outside the family. Family Rights Group also sees Family Group Conferences as a very useful model when consideration is being given to the permanent placement of children away from their parents. In such situations a Family Group Conference could first clarify whether there are placement options within the child's network, and could then address contact issues.

By using Family Group Conferences, contact plans can be made that reflect children's needs and families' resources. Family members have been able to provide appropriate supervision, comfortable venues, flexible transport and support for both the carers and the parents. Family Group Conferences help to move away from contact arrangements that are artificial and unhelpful. The model allows the particular patterns of a family to be recognised, and the full range of contact needs to be considered. Maintaining connections is rarely limited to a child being visited by their parents. Other adults, siblings and friends, particular places and activities are also important. Family plans enable these aspects to be included when contact arrangements are made.

Family Group Conferences will not be appropriate in every situation; a few families will fail to produce adequate plans. In such circumstances the professionals have a clear duty to act to promote the well-being of the child. Our experience to date indicates families rarely produce inappropriate or unsafe plans, and experience in New Zealand suggests very few Family Group Conferences result in the family plan being rejected or deemed unsafe.

Conclusion

This chapter has argued the need to avoid the professionalisation of contact arrangements. It has suggested that when models such as Family Group Conferences are used, families can and do produce appropriate plans. However, professionals do not have to adopt Family Group Conferences to achieve better contact plans. By consulting extended family members and friends, by encouraging parents and carers to plan together, and by demonstrating a commitment to arrangements that reflect the needs and circumstances of children and their families, the depressing and stressing experiences of too many children and their families can be avoided.

References

1. Hess P M, and Proch K O, *Contact: Managing visits to children looked after away from home*, BAAF, 1993.

2. Department of Health, *Patterns and Outcomes in Child Placement: Messages from current research and their implications*, HMSO, 1991.

3. Ward H, *Looking after Children: Research into practice*, HMSO, 1995.

4. Lindley B, *On the Receiving End: A qualitative study of families' experiences of the court process*, FRG, 1995.

5. Tunnard J, *Family Group Conferences*, A report commissioned by the Department of Health, FRG, 1994.

6. See '*Family Group Conferences*', issues 1–6, FRG.

12 Grandparents speak

Noreen Tingle

Noreen Tingle is the National Secretary of the Grandparents' Federation, which offers advice and support to grandparents who have young relations in care.

Curiosity, I recognise, is one of the reasons I can steel myself to keep hearing and reading about the fearful anguish that so many grandparents have to bear. They have different stories to tell, but they are all variations on a theme: their lack of contact with their grandchildren. I share their pain, offer a willing ear and try to analyse and make sense of the difficulties these grieving people are having to face. Sometimes it is relatively easy to discover what has gone wrong because there is a recognisable pattern of events leading to the problem. At other times, one is faced with a jigsaw without a pattern for guidance; it is then by chance that one finds the route which allows the various segments of the puzzle to be put together and into perspective. The problems some grandparents have about contact with their grandchildren who have the misfortune to be accommodated or to be in the care of the local authority, come under my heading of "difficult pieces" in a three dimensional jigsaw: local authority, family, and children.

As we are the National Grandparents' Federation, it is inevitable that the grandparents who come to us are anxious about some aspect of their young relatives' care. We must therefore assume that we do not see the whole picture. The Federation deals with people whose difficulties stem from either private or public family law; however, the issues which arise about contact are very similar in both spheres. If I can put forward an explanation for the possible causes of the problems over contact with grandchildren, then there is hope for a solution. But there are times when I have to help grandparents to accept that "playing the waiting game" and getting on with their lives as best they can is the only solution. This situation is made even harder when grandparents have to live with the fear that their grandchildren are missing them as much.

The special love between a grandparent and grandchild makes lack of contact between the two so desperately painful.

In the early 1980s, it became increasingly clear that many children were being adopted from care because they had completely lost contact with their families of birth. And even if parents were aware of the plans, there was rarely a legal route for the wider family's views to be heard on contact. The Grandparents' Federation, alongside other organisations, fought a hard campaign in the mid-1980s to achieve official recognition for the contact needs of children in care. It was an exhilarating time, for as someone remarked, 'You have right on your side'.

So it was that during 1989, a large crowd assembled to hear about the recommendations of the Children Bill. David Mellor, then Minister of Health, was at the last moment unable to be present to make the speech and Rupert Hughes from the Department of Health stood in for him. We waited expectantly, and a great cheer went up when we heard him state that contact with children in care was to be enshrined in the legislation. Our strivings for such children were over. Or so we thought . . . !

The biggest hitch, once the Children Act 1989 had been implemented, was that it takes more than a change in the law to change people. Human beings have their own personal agendas which are often in conflict with each other, and at the the root of many difficulties, is an inability to communicate effectively.

It is wholly regrettable that social workers have such a bad press and that the good they do goes unreported. But it is therfore not surprising that family members may more or less anticipate trouble from workers and, having got into entrenched positions, they show themselves in the worst possible light. Social workers may conclude that the relatives of these children are disruptive and could be an unsettling influence on the child. Almost inevitably, it is then considered necessary for contact to be supervised. This, in turn, frequently has the effect of limiting the contact for purely logistical reasons.

This was illustrated by a particular case of grandparents who came to the Federation because their grand-daughter, whom they had virtually brought up since birth, had been taken into local authority accommodation. The child had been non-accidentally injured while staying with her young mother, but once out of hospital, the grandparents had been allowed to take her home. They planned to go on holiday and were all but ready to leave when social workers came to remove the child. Understandably the grandparents objected strongly and an awful scene ensued. What the social workers did not explain was that their own daughter had not wanted them to take her child on holiday. The mother's wish prevailed because the child was not the subject of a care order; the mother held parental responsibility, and the workers were respecting her right to decide what she wanted for her daughter. Subsequently a care order was made and the poor grandparents were given supervised contact, once a month. It was left to a worker in the Grandparents' Federation to sort out the mistrust and misunderstandings with the manager of Children's Services in the area. Once this was done, the local authority quickly arranged for the grandparents to be assessed as carers for the child. Would that many others had such support.

The importance of "parental responsibility" is stressed in the 1989 Children Act. This is, of course, in general a good principle and one rightly emphasised by social workers. Sometimes though, what we hear from grandparents makes us realise that the principle can make children come a poor second best, as in the following account.

There were two children who had always been very close to their grandparents – the closeness turned into dependence when their single mother became hooked on drugs and alcohol. Social workers were left in no doubt that the grandparents would willingly look after the children, but the mother objected to such an arrangement. The children were accommodated in foster care, as the mother wished, but worse was to follow. She next objected to the children staying with the grandparents at weekends, and the social worker acceded to the mother's, by now drug crazed demands, that the children should have no contact at all with their grandparents. What kind of reasoning is it that makes workers decide that "parental rights" must override young children's needs and deny them the only source of stability they have ever known? Fortunately, a judge took little time to decree that the primary right for these two children was to have contact with their grandparents. Thank goodness for contact orders!

There are occasions when contact arrangements defy any logical explanation: consider the case of the African Carribean grandmother who was a Jehovah's witness. She was concerned that the hair of her grandchildren in care was becoming completely out of control. So she offered to make her weekly visit at a time when the children were to have their hair washed. She would then be able to show the foster carer how to plait and dress the hair, so that it would stay smart throughout the week. But this was not to be; she was informed by letter that the contact arrangements were proving too complicated for the foster carer; from henceforth, contact would be on Sunday mornings at a venue in the town. Obviously, hairdressing was not to be on the agenda; nor was our member's attendance at church which meant so much to her.

We never did get to the bottom of what went so badly wrong with these contact arrangements. Taken at face value, it could easily be thought that both foster carer and social worker had "a down" on this woman. The fact that no explanations were forthcoming left us wondering about several possibilities – any of which could have been true or false. The most worrying aspect of the situation was that the interests of the children were certainly not being given priority. The grandmother had wanted to be helpful but she was misunderstood. After this incident, the foster carers had their answerphone switched on all the time, so our member never actually spoke to them again. This case not only highlights once more the necessity for proper channels of communication, but also for a proper understanding and recognition of cultural differences.

We do not have many members from minority ethnic communities in the Grandparents' Federation. Why this is, we really don't know. Certainly, all people who contact us are welcomed as grandparents – any other criterion is irrelevant. However, one of our black members stands out a mile for sheer grit and determination to keep in touch with her grandchild who was adopted from care. When the adoption application was heard, our grandmother was there, battling to have contact with her adored grand-daughter. The judge said to her: 'Well now, your grandchild is to be adopted, and it is up to you to get on with the adoptive parents and sort out contact arrangements'. So it was that the first year on the afternoon of December 25th saw this grandmother sitting with her grandchild. Despite it being the season of goodwill, barely a word was spoken to her. Although she felt uncomfortable, she put such feelings to one side and concentrated on her grandchild. She kept up her visits, even if the reception from the family was anything but warm, her mind firmly on her grand-daughter's need to know her own grandmother. And now, three years later, the last thing we heard was that the adoptive family was taking our member on holiday with them.

Happily, examples of successful contact after adoption are becoming more usual; we have members whose contact with their adopted grandchildren far exceeds all they had hoped for. One set of grandparents sees their grandchildren six times a year, and lately, the children's mother has been invited to share the contact. Interestingly, this satisfactory state of affairs has developed in spite of the social workers who recommended no contact at all.

So there are still obstacles to overcome. In another instance, although a court directed that a couple should make a positive contribution to their grandson's adoptive placement, this was not allowed to happen by the adopters. The grandparents realised that taking the matter back to court would hardly cement good relationships, but what alternative did they have, knowing that their grandchild believed they would be visiting? This sad story clearly indicates that either the prospective adoptive family did not have sufficient preparation, or the workers were completely taken in by their apparent goodwill.

The Grandparents' Federation firmly believes that prospective carers, including adopters, should undergo training to enable them to acknowledge that every child placed in a substitute family also has a birth family which cannot be marginalised out of existence. This is especially important for children who have known their birth families. Nothing may be more essential for a child than to stay in touch with a loved grandparent. The continuity of the generations can offer reassurance to children who have been removed from their birth parents, and life story books are a rather poor substitute for children who could enjoy the advantage of hearing the family history from grandparents. Sometimes grandparents, who after all are not responsible for the family break-up, and so are not overwhelmed with guilt, are best able to help children come to terms with new situations. They can remind their grandchildren that no family is wholly bad and that even neglectful or abusing parents may once have been loving sons and daughters. They can demonstrate that although they cannot care *for* the children, this does not mean that they do not care *about* them. The role of grandparents should be valued for its own sake; not all grandparents can or wish to become full time substitute parents.

It would be unrealistic to imagine that contact with grandparents is, without exception, in the interests of every child in the care system, or that contact with grandparents can invariably be arranged, even when it would be desirable. And contact for grandparents is not always a straightforward affair. It can happen that parents are not allowed to visit but grandparents are. They are then torn by conflicting loyalties: they want to share the children with their son or daughter, but they also want to protect the children and to go on seeing them. It is a desperately sad situation, which gets worse as the grandparents get older. Encouragement, recognition and support from social workers will help grandparents to play their significant part in child care, even in the most unpromising circumstances.

Children themselves, of course, are not without the means of making some form of contact, once they have mastered the way. If they can use a telephone, they will. If they can write, they will. If they are old enough to get on a bus or a train, they will make the journey. In other words: they will vote with their feet. And for the grandparents I exhorted to be patient and to 'play the waiting game', what could be more truly wonderful than to hear the child's voice on the phone, to recognise the child's writing on the envelope, or to respond to a knock on the door: 'Hello Gran, it's only me!' Only? The one and only. It's your grandchild, and each one is uniquely precious.

13 Working in partnership with "lost" parents

Christine Harrison and Anita Pavlovic

Christine Harrison is a qualified social worker and a lecturer in Applied Social Studies at Warwick University. She is a Project Director of the Working in Partnership with "Lost" Parents research project.

Dr Anita Pavlovic is the Research Fellow for the Working in Partnership with "Lost" Parents research project and teaches in the Department of Applied Social Studies.

This chapter explores the relationship between two difficult and contentious concepts – partnership and contact – and examines their significance for children and young people being looked after by local authorities on a long-term basis. More specifically, it is about why and how social workers might re-establish working relationships with a group of parents we have called "lost" parents – parents whose children have been in care, probably for some time – and where there is currently no contact either between them and the local authority, or them and their children. Where there is neither partnership nor contact.

In trying to explore and define the relationship between "partnership" and "contact", a central organising feature and a thread running right through the discussion is the issue of identity for young people in care. We therefore ask how the relationship or lack of a relationship between partnership and contact impacts on a young person's developing sense of themselves and their individual, familial, cultural and ethnic identity, that is, how they answer questions about who they are.

What, why, and how?
The content of the chapter derives directly from an action-based research project funded by the Joseph Rowntree Foundation, *Working in Partnership with "Lost" Parents,* and an outline will be given of the focus for the research which is provided by the Children Act 1989. The rationale

is to be found in a diverse range of research, theoretical perspectives and personal accounts, which have accumulated with growing urgency during the 1970s, 80s and into the 90s. This diverse range of research, which can only be summarised here, informs current research and also provides a vital context against which to re-evaluate the care of children away from their families, partnership with parents, and the significance, form and extent of contact with parents and other people important to the child.

Our research project is not yet complete. However, in trying to identify what facilitates or impedes the restoration of working partnerships with "lost" parents, strong themes and issues have emerged which will be elaborated upon and the lives of some of the people involved will be introduced. For the research is very much about people's lives: what they are like now, what they might be like in the future, and in what ways parents might contribute to those lives, directly or indirectly.

What? The research focus

The importance of maintaining and promoting contact with parents, relatives, community and culture has been increasingly recognised as a crucial aspect of good child care practice when children are being looked after away from home. This is enshrined in the United Nations Conventions on the Rights of the Child and is endorsed by the Children Act 1989 and the guidance which accompanies it, with an explicit expectation that local authorities and voluntary organisations looking after children will work actively with parents and other significant people, even when children may not return to live with them. Parents now retain parental responsibility for their children even if a care order is made (S.33(3)) and local authorities should, where it is reasonably practicable, consult parents before making any decision and give due consideration to their wishes and feelings (S.22(4)) as well, of course, as to the wishes and feelings of the child or young person.

These provisions demand a high level of partnership between local authorities and parents and represent a new awareness of the contribution parents can make to a child's identity needs. They apply not only to children and young people brought into the care system since the implementation of the Children Act, but also to those children and young people who were already in care. Whilst partnership and contact are not synonymous, there is an undeniable relationship between them.

The focus of the research project is to examine how these aims for partnership can be realised with parents whose children have been in care for some time, probably since before the implementation of the Children Act – parents who have no current working relationship with the local authority and who have lost contact with their children.

This presents a major challenge to practice. Parents of children and young people in care have often experienced considerable disadvantage and discrimination. In the past parents have frequently been marginalised, their contribution to their child's development either undervalued or viewed as a destabilising influence.[1,2] They may have had little opportunity to participate in the lives of their children who entered care.[3,4] Some have experienced the guilt and depression associated with "filial deprivation" which can lead parents to give up trying to maintain contact with their children.[5] The result has been that in many cases either a parent's right of access has been terminated or has not been positively encouraged and has consequently foundered over the course of time. For some children and young people this, combined with their experiences of "care", has profoundly impaired their knowledge about their family and cultural history and their sense of self.

In 1990 there were over 25,000 children who had been in care for more than three years. This included 10,600 children under 16 who had been in care for more than five years and 16,400 who were the subjects of care orders.[6] A disproportionate number of these will be black children of African Caribbean parentage or black children of mixed parentage who are particularly over-represented in the long-term care population. It is difficult to estimate how many of these children and young people have lost a parent, although it is possible to estimate from the findings of Millham et al[7] that, for 7,000 of them, notices terminating access would have been served prior to the implementation of the Children Act. In addition, contact was probably interrupted without formal notice in twice as many cases.

There are likely to be significant numbers of situations where there is no active relationship between parents and children and no working relationship between parents and local authority. These are children and young people who have "holes in their history"[8] and where there may have been a lack of attention to an essential aspect of emotional health and development: a secure and positive sense of personal identity.

Why? The broader context of research and theory

The research focus arises from the legal imperatives of the Children Act, but to explore the practice imperatives we must go beyond legal provisions. A rationale for the research enterprise may be found in increasing and changing knowledge and understanding about why these particular changes were recommended and what they might mean for children and young people who are looked after.

Most children and young people who are looked after by local authorities go home; four out of five within weeks and nine out of ten within months. However, there has been accumulating evidence about the failings of the care system to provide good stable care for the small proportion of children and young people who remain looked after on an indefinite basis.[9] All too often, "care" is characterised by change and instability, or even abuse.[10] Attention has been drawn to the experiences and needs of black children and children with disabilities.[11,12,13] The effects of inadequacies in the care system are carried forward into adult life with resulting low self-esteem, depression, loneliness and isolation.[14,15]

Evidence has continued to accumulate about the impact of disadvantage and oppression in relation to gender, class, race, sexuality and disability. This is not just relevant in terms of how and why particular individuals and families become the subject of intervention, but because welfare agencies have failed to counteract the impact of oppression and have even compounded and perpetuated it.[16,17,18,19,20,21]

The relationship between parental contact and return home from care has been underlined.[22,23] Even where children and young people are unlikely to return home, the importance of birth family and other significant people to the well being of children, has been recognised.[24] In addition, the positive contribution contact can make to the stability of placements is acknowledged.[25,26] It is now more widely accepted that there are many routes to permanence[27,28] and that children can maintain attachments to a number of significant, parental figures in a complementary rather than competitive way.[29] Conversely, there is also a greater appreciation of how children with limited knowledge of their history and background, may be more likely to suffer identity crises during adolescence, leading to the disruption of what were previously thought to be successful placements.[30]

Research as well as theoretical and personal accounts have shifted views about attachment, permanence and the care of children separated from their families, and therefore about how contact is perceived. The impact on young people, of deliberately or inadvertently cutting them off from knowledge, information and connections with their personal history, has been reassessed. At the same time, the centrality of an analysis of disadvantage and the distribution of power urges practitioners away from a euphemistic use of the term partnership and towards a more empowerment based model.[31] As Dalrymple and Burke[32] argue 'True partnership means taking account of the power differentials and understanding the need to relinquish power. Partnership is an evolving negotiated process. It does not just happen, you have to work at it.'

Partnership is a way of working integral to anti-discriminatory practice. It does not, and maybe it should not, invariably lead to contact. However, it is perhaps the only gateway to positive and productive contact.*

How? The research process

Working in partnership with "lost" parents is a qualitative research project examining the work of social services departments in ten local authorities, looking at the lives of 50 children, one third of whom are black including those of mixed parentage. The project is exploring how links with lost parents can be established and what facilitates or impedes the re-establishment of working partnerships within an anti-oppressive framework. The progress and outcome of the work will draw on the perspectives of parents, children, young people, carers and social workers. It seeks to find out how and why contact ceased and if and how partner-

---

*Many of the principles defined in *Care of Children: Principles and practice in regulations and guidance*, DOH, 1989, which relate to identity, contact, partnership, etc., whilst too numerous to detail here, can be better understood with reference to this body of research.

ship might be related to contact in the future.

Early in the research process, response from fieldworkers confirmed that there are substantial numbers of children in care who have lost one or both parents or other family member; that these situations are exceptionally varied and complex; that they are not confined to pre-Children Act cases; that contact is put on the agenda by children and young people and that practitioners frequently feel fearful about how to proceed. A number of factors contribute to not knowing how to proceed.

Social workers are practising in a changing and difficult environment. Within teams, work with children and young people who are looked after long term is underrated, as child protection dominates professional concern and individual case loads. Sometimes a young person may not have an allocated worker for lengthy periods, or work may be restricted to a crisis or a prelude to change, for example, of placement.

Although the recognition of empowerment based approaches predates the Act, and has been embraced by many committed practitioners, it does, nevertheless, pose a challenge in relation to both existing or new cases. It is particularly daunting to contemplate developing a working relationship in situations where contact with a parent ceased some time ago, and where workers are struggling with the inheritance of different values, or bad, even discriminatory practice.

It must be remembered that parents were very often "lost" in an era when social work practice was different. In many of the cases in the study, access had been formally terminated, and even where this was not the case, parents had been excluded and discounted. Case records reveal that some mothers persisted for years in maintaining contact with the local authority, asking for information and providing information, cards and photographs, with little response or reassurance about what would happen to their contributions.

The current social workers' view may be that children in similar circumstances today would not be looked after. Neither are they always clear, in the light of changing philosophies and practices, why the child or young person has remained in care or why access was terminated. It is likely that some lost parents are unaware of even basic details, such as the legal status of their child, where parental rights were assumed with a plan for adoption which did not come to fruition.

If parents' whereabouts are unknown, their reactions cannot be anticipated. Perceptions of them contained within files may have been inaccurate then and be irrelevant now. In many instances, files reveal that parents received very little support at the time of the initial intervention and might now feel resentful, threatened or distressed by renewed intervention. Workers are aware that getting in touch may generate anger and grief which has remained unexpressed for years. Whilst having initiated contact primarily to meet the child or young person's needs, practitioners will then have to acknowledge and respond to parents' needs as well as those of present carers.

In early discussions with participating social workers, all of whom were committed to working in partnership, these factors, they felt, inhibited them from embarking on work which has to confront organisational and professional priorities. There is also ambivalence and fear of increasing complexity and conflict in already complex and conflictual situations.

From the first round of interviews and detailed reading of case records, some going back for eighteen years, it has been possible to plot an understanding of how and why the local authority's contact with a parent, and the parent's contact with a child, became lost.

How contact was lost
All of the children and young people in the study have lost contact with one or both of their parents. Many have also lost contact with their extended families, community and culture.

Some of the parents were lost before the child came into the care system, as the result of family breakdown or because a father had never been known. Other children and young people have become estranged from their families through being looked after, either because access was legally terminated or as a result of a lack of social work support for, or encouragement of, parental involvement. The provisions of the Children Act do not distinguish between these situations, but the process of estrangement can be very significant to whether, and how, contact might be re-established.

Neither becoming "lost" nor being "found" occur in a vacuum. Rather, both processes happen in the context of a broader familial, social, political arena and reflect changing and competing philosophies and practices.

> *'Our long-standing traditions of child rescue have meant that first Children's Departments and then Social Services Departments have tended to marginalise parents even when acting benevolently towards them. The strong emphasis on the welfare of the child has often pushed parents' needs and wishes into the background and departments have assumed full control of children admitted to their care and assumed they knew best.'[33]*

The influence of the tradition of child rescue is clearly documented in the case histories of children and young people in the study. Their files indicate that agencies have been prepared (or obliged) to employ harsh measures against specific sections of the population in order to "cover their own backs" against a wider attack from political sources.[34] Parental accounts of their actions have either been omitted from social work records or displaced in favour of competing explanations that have been elevated to the level of expertise.[35] These "expert" opinions have frequently been employed as the yardstick with which to measure and test parental commitment.

Case

> Jane was first received into care on a voluntary basis when she was aged four years, following her mother's admitted "inability to cope" with Jane's behaviour. The social work plan was to address these difficulties and work towards rehabilitation. Jane was placed with foster carers but had regular contact with her mother, including overnight stays. During one overnight stay, Jane protested that she was unhappy in her placement and, in response, her mother decided to resume Jane's care herself, against social work advice.
>
> Jane's mother was viewed as having no commitment to her, on the grounds that she disregarded social work decisions.
>
> Six months later, and with no interim support, Jane was again received into care. Because the professional view was that her mother

had "refused to heed advice" on the previous occasion, combined with anxieties that she might again remove Jane, wardship proceedings were instigated.

The Judge directed that her mother should have access to Jane "not less than four times a year" and leave was granted to place Jane with long-term carers. This time Jane's mother's compliance with the social work plan was interpreted as her "lack of interest and commitment to Jane" on the basis that she no longer questioned social work decisions, which were now leading towards long-term care.

It is within these constructions of "good" and "bad" parents, that birth families have frequently had access to their children terminated. (In Jane's case, access was eventually terminated because it was no longer happening and contact between Jane and her Mum had to be re-established after a nine year gap.) Even where termination of access was not formal, the discouragement of parental involvement, in favour of alternative substitute family care, has often ensured that contact was lost.

Some of the children and young people in the study have had an unsettled care career with multiple placements and a succession of social workers, combined with a severance of familial, cultural and community ties. This has resulted in difficulties in forming and maintaining both meaningful relationships and a positive self image. Either the threat to stability or the symptoms of instability can then provide the rationale for action (termination of access) or inaction (failure to encourage parental involvement) and render parents irrelevant.

Promoting contact

Re-establishing contact with lost parents presents both practical problems and ethical dilemmas for social workers. Tracing is often identified as the first barrier to establishing a working relationship with parents and to renewing contact between children and their families.

Case

Steven's parents had been lost to both him and the Department for almost eighteen years, when Steven requested that his social worker obtain knowledge and information about his family. The last known home of Steven's parents had been demolished some sixteen years ago. No extended family members were known to the Department. Steven's social worker did not know how to begin.

Case

Alex was received into care aged six months, following the death of his mother. Alex's father, on the advice of social workers at that time, had consented to Alex being placed for adoption. This never happened, but Alex's father was never informed that Alex remained in long-term care. Seventeen years later, Alex indicated to his social worker that he "wanted to know" about his family. The case worker was now faced with the task of locating Alex's father.

Most social workers in the study have been fascinated and enthused to learn about the tracing process, but have been denied the social work time and financial resources that are necessary to carry out what, at a managerial level, is not considered a legitimate social work activity. Even when parents are located, they might be reluctant to form a working relationship with agencies that previously denied them any articulate role in decision-making and discounted their views.

For social workers, obligations and priorities always relate to what is perceived and understood to be in the best interests of the child. Faced with what to do, if the child wants contact but the parent doesn't; if the parent wants contact but the child doesn't; if no-one has placed contact on the agenda but the case worker is aware of legal obligations, social workers will, not surprisingly, be cautious about taking risks.

Themes and issues

Although the lives of children and parents in the study show great diversity, issues emerging tend to cluster around several significant themes. These have both historical and contemporary dimensions. Historical, in the sense that they provide a longer term context against which the development of a case can be viewed and contemporary, in the sense that they do still exercise a powerful influence on current practice. Like the severance of access, the promotion of contact has to be analysed in relation to a broader canvas of social work and legal parameters, as well as to the value placed upon parents. If there are elements which shut the door on partnership and contact, they have to be counteracted for the door to be opened up again. Some of them represent themes which have proved difficult to challenge, despite the body of research alluded to earlier.

Defining partnership

The research to date has revealed that social workers have difficulty in devising an operational definition of "partnership". In practice, they tend to locate it along a continuum, with the notion (or anxiety) that "partnership impedes planning" at one end, and the view that "permanence inhibits creativity" at the other. These ideological foundations to the concept of partnership inform social work practice in very significant and powerful ways.

Striking a balance between the powers of social workers and the rights of children and parents demands a consultative approach, whereby parents of children being looked after have, at the very least, a right to be advised, consulted and informed about their children's welfare and development. Because the concept of partnership has a high level of use and a low level of meaning, it might be more helpful, in terms of practice, for social workers to concentrate on parental involvement.

Partnership and contact are synonymous in the minds of social workers
Partnership and contact are often conflated in the minds of social workers, who see their contact with a parent as being indistinguishable from a parent having contact of some description with a child. Two particular difficulties can result.

The first, a belief that partnership will invariably lead to contact, can generate a fear of the unknown, succinctly described by one research participant as like "opening up a can of worms". Once back on the scene a parent might want something or demand something. It might not be possible to control the situation, with the threat of disruption inspiring both professional and organisational panic. There is additional discomfort when case records indicate that a parent may have tried to sustain involvement, without encouragement, over many years and for whom renewed social work activity now, may represent a volte face for which current social workers must take responsibility.

It is a further inhibiting factor when a social worker possesses information about a child's development or situation which will be painful to share with a parent. Alex, for example, had several foster homes and has experienced emotional and sexual abuse whilst being in care. Once his father has been located, Alex's social worker has the unenviable prospect of conveying what happened during his care career.

Secondly, there are circumstances when partnership is viewed as an instrumental, expedient relationship through which something can be gained from a parent. A social worker may well be motivated by a desire to strengthen a child's sense of identity, to provide knowledge or information about family or cultural history, or to gain access to other people of significance to the child. Little consideration will be given to the broader requirements and principles of working in partnership and parents' needs and interests may be unacknowledged and ignored.

It is hard to accept and deal with potentially conflicting interests. It can become an attractive proposition to locate the problem with a parent and to resolve the legal–practice tension, by dismissing partnership as something not practicable or not in a child's interests. Conflating partnership and contact obscures aims and keeps doors firmly shut. Where the two can be conceptually separated, progress can be made. In Alex's case and others, social workers have given very careful attention about when and how to approach parents once found.

Steven's parents have been traced and an initial approach made by letter. Alex's father has been located and approached. Although seriously ill, distressed and angry about what has happened to Alex, he and Alex's social worker have been able to work together. He has written to Alex about how he and Alex's mother loved him when he was born and how he thought Alex would have a better life if he agreed to adoption. Miraculously, Alex's father had photographs and a baby book that his mother had compiled. Alex now has these and hopefully may meet again with his father.

Contact and rehabilitation are synonymous in the minds of social workers

Not only has partnership been conflated with contact, but the value of contact has been measured in relation to rehabilitation. Both partnership and contact have frequently been downgraded if rehabilitation is not seen to be a realistic possibility; this has generally been the basis for the low priority given to work with parents and the termination of access. A narrow conceptualisation of identity has construed contact, at best, as irrelevant if rehabilitation was not to take place and, at worst, counterproductive and diversionary, inhibiting planning and the real case work. Where either a parent or child has disabilities, it has sometimes been assumed that contact will be valueless and has therefore never even been considered.

Some children and young people in the study, whose placements were viewed as stable, became "back burner cases" or were unallocated. Work with them was not seen to be necessary unless some crisis precipitated it – work was about offsetting negative consequences, rather than promoting positive ones, on both ideological and organisational grounds.

Today, social workers are confronting the longer term consequences of this practice, either because the young person is vociferously demanding some kind of contact, or because they have themselves reappraised the value of contact for the young person's development and knowledge of themselves.

In one case, for example, a social worker who was involved in terminating access some eight years ago, has questioned the actions which not only denied a child information and access to his family but also, as a black child placed transracially with a white family, to the black community. She has painstakingly undertaken work with the young person, searched for family members, re-established contact with siblings – all on a careful, planned basis and with a tenacity and commitment which have effectively counterbalanced the long shadows cast by previous decisions.

Nothing worse will happen or nothing will happen anyway

There are some circumstances where partnership with a view to contact is relatively elevated in the work but not necessarily for positive reasons.

It may be that a child's experiences of care have already been so disruptive, that re-establishing contact with a parent does not hold the same kind of threat; that the chances of finding one or both parents are thought to be low, or there is a belief that parents will not respond or will not manage to maintain involvement.

You're either a parent or you're not

Parenthood in this society is constructed in such a way that it comprises an exclusive set of responsibilities, whereas in some other societies, tasks, roles and responsibilities associated with caring for children are more broadly distributed and undertaken. The consequences of having failed to discharge parental responsibilities are costly and, certainly in the past, disqualification from parenting has meant playing no part in a child's life and development. Negative judgements about having failed as a parent, combined with a difficulty in conceiving of any role for a parent with a looked after child, leave little space for a parent to occupy legitimately.

Without a readily available cultural script, social workers may have to invent one, and undertake the difficult task of creating the opportunity for parents, who do not have day to day care, to be involved in some other way in a child's life. The Children Act redefines parental responsibility, but this will mean little without an accompanying shift in values and practice.

Being a parent

Arguably, working in partnership with parents is a pre-requisite for the sharing of parental responsibility required when children are looked after by local authorities. However, the concept of "parent" used within the legislation is gender-neutral. In reality, of course, parental roles are largely based on a gendered division of labour and when we separate the elements of parental responsibility into rights, duties and powers, it becomes clear that "parents" are not only gendered but unequal.

Women, as primary carers, are expected to ensure that children are cared for and protected in terms of their personal and developmental needs. These expectations are combined with assumptions about, for example, a mother's sexuality and marital status and are applied whatever the woman's circumstances. In reality, the labour of caring for children often consists of daily routines, in an isolated environment and within a set of social relations, which render women invisible and power-less. This has particular implications for black mothers, lesbian mothers and lone mothers. Intra-household poverty,[36] racism, domestic vio-lence,[37] and poor physical and emotional health,[38,39] are prominent features in the lives of many women and children.

The individualised nature of social work intervention has tended to dislocate motherhood, in particular, from its operational moorings. Both at the time of initial intervention and at later stages, parental actions will be heavily interpreted according to the dominant and Eurocentric familial ideologies on which the principle of parental responsibility is based. The case examples from our research demonstrate the contradic-tions between what is expected of parents, and the realities of women's lives which have been crucial in terms of caring for children. The pro-cesses of intervention have not only failed to resolve these contradictions but have compounded them.

Case

Andrea's mother was living in a violent relationship. In an attempt to protect herself and Andrea, she applied for an injunction to exclude her partner from her home. In court, Andrea's mother found that rather than being seen as protecting her children, she was viewed as having failed to protect Andrea who was made the subject of a care order and placed in local authority care. Although the local authority success-fully appealed against the order, Andrea remained in care, her mother's confidence and ability to care for her undermined by both her experiences at the hands of her partner and the agencies to which she turned for assistance.

Case

Suzanne's mother had been subjected to extreme physical abuse for many years and had frequently attempted to escape from this violence with her three children. Her partner had seriously injured her, but when he applied for legal custody of Suzanne, she withdrew her objections after he inflicted further injuries. She was too frightened to draw this to the attention of agencies and somehow their inquiries failed to reveal it. Subseqently, Suzanne was removed from her father after she was physically and sexually abused and the longer history of violence was exposed. By this time Suzanne's mother had placed her other two children in care, as she felt they would always be at risk of violence whilst they lived with her. Suzanne has effectively lost her mother and siblings.

Carrying more responsibility means taking more of the blame, irrespective of the factors or who is actually at fault. Having failed as a parent has adhesive qualities more likely to stick to women than to men. Fathers are lost to children too, of course, and many of the children in the study would welcome information and contact with them. However, the value that children and young people might place on locating or approaching a father is not always evident from either social work practice or case histories. The ways in which fathers become "lost" are very often strikingly different from how mothers become lost.

Substitute family care

The same familial ideology, against which the actions of birth parents, particularly mothers, will be measured, influences the provision of substitute family care. Foster carers are by definition better parents and the notion of the sharing of parental responsibility (whether through informing or involving or consulting) is embedded in unequal power relationships – not just between workers and parents but between carers and parents.

Placement stability is an overriding consideration for social workers who may fear that working in partnership with parents will threaten placements. Some foster carers, themselves grappling with changing philosophies, find the idea of shared parental responsibility problematic and also assume that partnership means direct contact between parent and child. This can increase the sense of divided loyalties that children often feel, wanting to know about themselves but not wanting to offend when contact is under discussion.

By virtue of their privileged position in being not just better parents but a scarce resource, precedence is easily given to the views of carers who, whether they are aware of it or not, have considerable power in relation to both social workers and parents. This is exemplified, at perhaps its most extreme, by two cases in the study where children in care believe they are the carers' birth children.

In practice, it can mean that when a child or young person is in foster care, there is fear leading to an assumption that working with parents will generate conflict. But where social workers and carers have acknowledged the relevance of partnership and encouraged direct or indirect parental involvement, then a contribution has indeed been made to placement stability.

Summary

There are many themes and issues which are relevant as we try to disentangle and understand partnership and contact for the sake of children who are looked after.

There are cases in the study where parents have indicated that they do not want to have contact with either the social worker or their child. There are examples of contact or access being terminated in reaction to serious child protection issues. Even then, neither partnership nor contact should be ruled out, but rather, careful consideration given to how they could be promoted, re-established and managed.

Within the context of both the parameters of social work practice and an analysis of social divisions, most "lost" parents might perhaps more aptly describe themselves as excluded parents who, through their powerlessness, have lost any kind of relationship with their children.

Conclusions

The retrospective application of the Children Act presents difficulties for social work policy and practice. In many respects, working in partnership with lost parents merely intensifies the issues that partnership evokes whenever children are being looked after and parental responsibility is shared.

The research project is founded on an accumulating knowledge base which represents changing views about permanence, contact and the significance of birth families and wider social and cultural networks for a child's identity. Whilst the children and young people discussed here form only a small proportion of the long-term care population, comparatively little attention has been paid to their quality of life.[40] The personal map of identity is formed in a social and political climate. For many young people care is a stigmatising and disruptive experience which compounds other experience of oppression – poverty, racism, homophobia, sexism.

Partnership and contact are not synonymous. Although either or both may ultimately benefit a child or young person, they need to be disaggregated and their form and content related to an active and positive approach to a child's needs.

It is clearly difficult to translate theory into practice. Legislation can give direction, but does not address the complexities of an individual's situation. Neither can it find the answers about how to develop positive practice in agencies where child protection concerns dominate professional discourse.

However, powerful incentives are found not just within the research but within the narratives of lives like Denise, Alex, Steven and Suzanne. Although simplistic remedies are not available, the dominant inhibiting themes can be identified and challenged and if more marginal voices are centralised, then dramatic things can happen. The significance to a child or young person of something as small as a description, a photograph or a piece of handwriting, should never be underestimated and can literally mean the world to them.

References

1. Masson J, 'Access disputes between parents and children in the long-term care of others,' *International Journal of Family Law*, 4, 1990.

2. Department of Health, *Patterns and Outcomes in Child Placement*, HMSO, 1991.

3. Family Rights Group, *Promoting Links: Keeping children and families in touch*, London, FRG.

4. Fisher M, Marsh P, Phillips D, and Sainsbury E, *In and Out of Care: The experiences of children, parents and social workers*, BAAF/Batsford, 1986.

5. Jenkins S, and Norman E, *Filial Deprivation and Foster Care*, Columbia University Press, 1972, USA.

6. Department Of Health, *Children in Care of Local Authorities: Year ending 31 March 1991*, HMSO, 1991.

7. Millham S, Bullock R, Hosie K, and Little M, *Access Disputes in Child Care*, Aldershot, Gower, 1989.

8. Barthel J, *For the Children's Sake: The promise of family preservation*, McConnell Clark Foundation, 1991, USA.

9. See 2 above.

10. Morris S, and Wheatley H, *Time to Listen: The experiences of children in residential and foster care*, Childline, 1994.

11. Barn R, *Black Children in the Public Care System*, BAAF/Batsford, 1993.

12. Banks N, 'Techniques for direct identity work with black children', *Adoption & Fostering*, 16:3, BAAF, 1992.

13. Morris J, *Gone Missing? A research and policy review of disabled children living away from their families,* Who Cares? Trust, 1995.

14. Stein M, and Carey K, *Leaving Care*, Blackwell, 1986.

15. Biehal N, Claydon J, Stein M, and Wade T, *Prepared for Living? A survey of young people leaving the care of three local authorities*, National Children's Bureau, 1992.

16. Ahmad B, *Black Perspectives in Social Work*, Venture Press, 1990.

17. Langan M (ed), *Women, Oppression and Social Work*, Routledge, 1992.

18. See 11 above.

19. Rights of Women Lesbian Custody Group, *Lesbian Mother's Legal Handbook*, Rights of Women, 1986.

20. Booth T, and Booth W, *Parenting under Pressure: mothers and fathers with learning difficulties*, Open University Press, 1994.

21. See 13 above.

22. Millham S, Bullock R, Hosie K, and Haak M, *Lost in Care: The problem of maintaining links between children in care and their families*, Gower, 1986.

23. Bullock R, Little M, and Millham S, *Going Home: the return of children separated from their families*, Aldershot, Dartmouth, 1994.

24. Haimes R, and Timms N, *Adoption, Identity and Social Policy*, Gower, 1985.

25. Fanshel D, and Shinn E B, *Children in Foster Care: A logitudinal study*, Columbia University Press, 1987, USA.

26. Berridge D, and Cleaver H, *Foster Home Breakdown*, Blackwell, 1987.

27. Triseliotis J, 'Adoption with contact', *Adoption & Fostering*, 9:4, BAAF, 1985.

28. Thoburn J, *Success and Failure in Permanent Family Placements*, Gower, 1990.

29. Schaffer R, *Making Decisions about Children: Psychological questions and answers*, Blackwell, 1990.

30. Howe D, and Hinings D, 'Adopted children referred to a child and family centre', *Adoption & Fostering*, 11:3, 44, BAAF, 1987.

31. Rees S, *Achieving Power: Practice and policy in social welfare*, Allen and Unwin, 1991, Australia.

32. Dalrymple J, and Burke B, *Anti-oppressive Practice: Social care and the law*, Open University Press, 1995.

33. See 2 above.

34. Carlan P, 'Pindown, truancy and the interrogation of discipline: A paper about theory, policy, social worker bashing . . . and hypocrisy', *Journal of Law and Society*, 19:2 Summer 1992.

35. Coombe V, and Little A, *Race and Social Work*, Tavistock, 1986.

36. Pahl J, *Money and Marriage*, Macmillan Educational, 1989.

37. Dobash R, and Dobash R, *Women, Violence and Social Change*, Routledge, 1992.

38. Bernard J, *The Future of Marriage*, Souvenir Press, 1973.

39. Graham H, *Hardship And Health In Women's Lives*, Harvester Wheatsheaf, 1993.

40. Stevenson O, 'Social Work Interventions to Protect Children: Aspects of research and practice', *Child Abuse Review*, 1: 19–32, 1992.

14 Looking to the future
Planning for permanence

Margaret Adcock

Margaret Adcock is a Social Work Consultant.

In the first chapter, the difficulties in providing good quality care for children away from home and in maintaining links with absent parents were noted. The introduction of each major new piece of child care legislation had been accompanied by a hope that in future things would be different and better for children and families. Each time the research suggested that in general this had not happened.

Recent studies now suggest that too much attention in social services departments is being directed at initial child protection investigations.[1] There is still the preoccupation with early decisions which was identified in the research published in 1984.

There is as yet no major research to tell us what is happening to children who have entered the care system since the introduction of the Children Act 1989. Such a study is urgently needed. Impressionistically, many practitioners feel that although there may be more parental contact, services for children living in their families and for children who are looked after by the local authority have not improved and indeed may have deteriorated. There are not enough preventive services to improve the quality of family life and the care of children. Family placement workers describe huge shortage of resources, inappropriate placement of children, rapid turnover of placements, high breakdown rate, and lack of time and services for both children, their carers and their birth families.

Although there have been different approaches to the provision of services over the years, there has been considerable agreement throughout about what was the central problem. In 1985, in the Department of Health report, Rowe[2] commented:

'The prevailing picture of drift, passivity and lack of planning is

pervasive and clearly not conducive to child welfare.'

It has led to 'hundreds of thousands of children in "temporary care" for the greater part of their childhoods, suffering multiple foster moves and the consequent destruction of their ability to form normal attachments.'[3]

Failure to develop secure attachments and the experience of emotional abuse and neglect can lead to many problems later, such as developmental delay, depression, poor peer relationships and aggressive and anti-social behaviours. Perhaps the major way in which local authorities may cause harm to children for whom they have responsibilities, is by ignoring the importance of attachment and attachment theory.

Maintaining parental contact is not in itself sufficient to compensate for lack of planning, frequent care episodes and multiple moves. Every professional and every manager needs to understand the importance of attachment for children's healthy growth and development and to act on this knowledge in working with children and families, and in making plans and contact arrangements. The aim of this chapter is to explore a framework for planning care and managing contact which will facilitate the development of healthy attachments.

Why is attachment so important?

There is general agreement amongst clinicians and researchers that all children need a secure attachment (see Chapter 3 by Lindsey). Attachment in childhood is formed through a consistent daily caretaking relationship between an adult and a child. A limited range of familiar people should provide consistent care throughout the years of childhood.[4] The adult's ability to be aware of and respond sensitively to the child's needs is the key factor.

'The attachment dynamic appears to be universal, a species characteristic of human beings. Clearly culture makes a difference. Cultural differences, however, take the form of degree and style of this behaviour. What has significance are patterns of mutuality and comfort that give the child security, not narrowly defined behaviour.'[5]

What is noticeable over time about a normal parent-infant relationship is its reciprocal nature and its continuity over time regardless of the child's culture.

Field[6] has defined the formation of an attachment as a relationship that develops between two or more organisms as their behavioural and physiological systems become attuned to each other. Each partner provides meaningful stimulation for the other; each partner has a modulating effect on the other's arousal level. The relationship facilitates an optimal growth state; this is threatened by changes in the individuals, their relationship, or by separation. According to Perry,[7] the early caregiving relationship – its synchrony with the infant, effectiveness in soothing the child and the stimulation it provides – all have a major impact on the early organisation of the brain. Perry suggests that consistency, predictability and nurturance are the three necessary conditions for brain development.

The child who has secure attachments will develop what Erickson[8] called a "sense of basic trust". This will enable the child to move into subsequent developmental stages. Poor inconsistent care and or multiple placements may undermine the child's ability to move into subsequent stages. Gradually the child develops a sense of identity – who they are, how they see themselves and how others see them. If previous experiences have been inconsistent and/or harmful, children may be confused, lack self-esteem, and have difficulties in developing a secure identity.

Providing a care system that facilitates attachments

Preventive services and the care system need to ensure that the child is provided with experiences which help to maintain or develop good attachments leading to self esteem and a secure identity.

Katz[9] suggests that the care system must change its purpose from protection and substitute care to an emphasis on continuity of care. The aim of services must be to maintain the continuity of care – which moves from the birth family, through out of home placement, and ends with the return to the birth family, kinship care or placement in an adoptive family. The focus of work is towards the preservation of families. The goal of the work must be the permanence and maintenance of attachments. Family reunification, kinship care or adoption can all be considered as successful outcomes to temporary care as they have the potential to give the child continuity of care and permanence.

What does planning for continuity of care involve?

This kind of planning has been defined by Maluccio[10] as

'the systematic carrying out, within a brief time-limited period, of a set of goal-directed activities designed to help children live in families that offer continuity of relationships with nurturing parents or caretakers and the opportunity to establish lifetime relationships.'

These activities are not new and have been advocated for many years in government guidance.

Kagan and Schlosberg[11] have suggested that every plan for a child looked after by a local authority should be scrutinised to see how it meets their attachment needs. A plan, to be successful, requires a series of activities. These have been described by Katz[12] as:

– A high level of systematic, goal-directed activity from social workers and other professionals. This requires the commitment and support of managers. It needs to be an organisational as well as an individual worker activity.

– Work with birth parents that nurtures parents in order to help them nurture their children. Crittenden[13] warns against

'ignoring the victimisation of most maltreating parents by their own parents and by a culture that devalues them. If parents are treated in the same coercive manner in which they were treated as children and now treat their own children, treatment providers become part of the dysfunctional approach they are trying to correct.'

– Work needs to be culturally sensitive. Parents need to be involved in the decison-making and to be given candid feedback from their worker throughout the process. Parents need to be told what we know about the negative effects of substitute care on children.[14]

– Accurate assessment. Katz suggests that the basis of good planning is differential diagnosis of the family's strengths and deficits. The central problem, the condition which, if not corrected, will prevent reunification, must be identified.

- Immediate efforts to contact relatives who might provide support to the family and/or placement for the child so that case planning can begin with them.
- Sharing the assessment results with the family and developing a time-limited service plan, based on written agreements, and focussing first on the central problem which needs to be resolved.
- Developing a contact plan based on the child's age and developmental level that ensures frequent meaningful contact.
- If the differential diagnosis determines the chances of rehabilitation are poor, the worker begins the discussion of a permanent relative or adoption placement.

If the parents have not made progress within the time allowed, the worker takes steps to implement the alternative plan for the child.

For younger children, where the chances of helping the parent(s) to change seem small, Katz[15] recommends placing the child with carers whom she calls "permanency planning foster parents". They are assessed and prepared as both foster and adoptive parents and are asked to commit themselves to seeing a child all the way through to permanency. They are trained to assist in working towards rehabilitation but if rehabilitation fails, are willing to keep the child on a permanent adoptive basis thereafter. This is an extension of the current practice of foster parent adoption and it preserves the continuity of attachments that is so necessary for children.

Although permanency planning activity has always been directed mainly at younger children, older children and young people in care also have needs for good attachments and continuity of care. Many of the professional tasks described by Katz[16] are appropriate for adolescents. Work needs to be undertaken to provide adolescents who are away from their birth families with good quality care, stability and attachment figures (although it is unlikely that adoption would be a relevant solution). There needs also to be an emphasis on preserving the continuity with birth families so that they can provide an appropriate secure base from which the young person can move towards increasing independence, but to which they can return for comfort, support and encouragement in their adult lives. This means work to try to resolve some of the problems that led to the young person leaving home in the first instance.

Contact

Planned and well managed contact is an essential part of achieving the goals of maintaining continuity and providing permanence. The contact plan must be part of and reflect the overall plan. Much of the work to achieve the overall goals may take place during contact visits.

The contact plan should specify the following:
- tasks that are to be accomplished during visits
- the frequency, venue and length of visits
- who is to participate in the visit
- if and how visits are to be supervised
- agency and parental responsisbilities related to visits.

(See also Chapter 5 by Newman)

Hess[17] relates the purpose and nature of contact to the stages of a care plan. As the plan progresses through its stages it must be reviewed, and at this review decisions about the nature and purpose of contact appropriate to the next stage must be taken.

Initially the purpose is to sustain existing relationships *and* to assess the parent–child relationship and the parent's ability to care for and relate to the child. This facilitates a differential diagnosis and identification of the main obstacles to reunification.

In the next phase the aim is to encourage change, using contact to help the parents develop appropriate parenting behaviours, to help the child interact with the parents, to attempt to resolve problems before the child returns home and to evaluate the family's progress towards agreed targets. This enables an assessment to be made of the feasibility and timing of the child's return home. It is likely to require intensive involvement from the carers, as well as other professionals, to help parents to develop new skills.

Contact arrangements then need to ease the child's transition to the parents' home. Again, this usually requires considerable involvement from the carers to assist in transferring attachments. Contact with the carers may need to go on for months or even years, so that the child does not suffer from the loss of one important attachment figure in the effort to keep hold of another. Some parenting from both may be desirable in the sense that it is preferable to extend rather than to transfer attachments when children move.

If it is decided that rehabilitation is not the goal, contact needs to be used to assist family members to deal with the planned adjustment in their relationship, whether or not there is a plan for continuing contact in the future. Both parents and children may need help in grieving for their lost hope for a family life together. It is very important for the child that, if possible, the parent(s) can explain the reasons for this and can give the child permission to live in another family.

It is vital to assess the capacity of the child, the birth parents and other family members, and of the alternative parents to cope with contact at any point in time. Situations and feelings may change. Some children at certain stages in their life may not wish to see their birth parents. For example, Jean who left her birth family when she was eight, continued to see her birth father until she was 13. At this point, her father remarried and indicated to Jean that he thought she should return home. Jean was exceedingly unhappy about this suggestion and refused to see him. Discussions and life story work went on for a year or two, and she finally said that she thought she would see her father when she was in her late teens. She felt she would then be stronger and better able to cope with the relationship. She was quite clear that she did not wish the relationship to stop completely but she had no desire for contact meanwhile.

Triseliotis[18] suggests that the way the adults relate to each other will have a powerful effect on whether contact is beneficial to the child. Social workers and other professionals are very influential in this process. They need to be aware that the goal is for the child to be able to achieve attachment and a sense of belonging in a new family whilst maintaining links with the family of origin in a way that enhances self-esteem and a good sense of identity. They need to recognise the needs and the vulnerability of both sets of adults and try to help them to work together for the benefit of the child. The worker who identifies pre-dominantly with one or other set of adults is not likely to help the child.

Experience in mediation in divorce suggests that a considerable amount of input may be necessary to help the adults come to an agreement that everyone is able to adhere to. The context for these agreements is crucial. An adoptive father who had negotiated a very successsful agreement with the birth mother of his child said that he felt that it was important that there was mutual respect and liking, that there was recognition about who held the legal parenting responsibilities, that there was agreement about what to do if contact arrangments seemed not to be working, and that the adults involved were flexible. Creating such a context is often very hard work.

Can continuity of care be achieved?

Social workers and others have many skills and are very familiar with the activities that have been outlined as necessary to achieve continuity of care and permanence for children. Why then is it so difficult to do what is needed?

It seems that at the moment organisations and individuals mirror many of the problems in the families they work with. Achieving continuity of care requires an understanding and acceptance of its importance for children and young people. Departmental policies seem to change regularly, reorganisations are frequent and social workers and managers change posts often. This has meant that there is no organisational or personal continuity for staff, children and families; there is often no transmission of important theoretical knowledge, or of what has actually happened to children and families, which would illustrate the theory, and enable the development of new understandings. This has been clearly demonstrated by small local research projects.

Little official recognition has been given to the importance of professionals offering parents and carers consistency, predictability and nurturance, so that they themselves can provide these essential elements for children. Good professional help, like good parenting, requires time and attention to detail.

Following the recent Department of Health research,[19] local authorities are now being asked to reconsider the way in which they intervene in families and to try and increase support and help for parents. There are many, often quite small, changes that could be made if everyone at all levels in an organisation understood and was committed to promoting attachments and continuity of care and was required and ennabled to put their understanding into practice. This seems an appropriate time to try and improve what is offered to children.

References

1. Department of Health, *Child Protection: Messages from Research*, HMSO, 1995.

2. Rowe J (ed), *Social Work Decisions in Child Care: Recent research findings and their implications*, Department of Health and Social Security, 1985.

3. Katz L, *Concurrent Planning: From permanency planning to permanency action*, Lutheran Social Services, 1994, USA.

4. Ball C, and Berkley Hill B, *The Welfare of Children Workbook 2, The Welfare of the Child: Assessing evidence in children cases,* published on behalf of the Magistrates Association by the Learning Business, 1994.

5. See 3 above.

6. Field T, 'Attachment as Psychological Attunement: Being on the same wavelength', in *The Psychobiology of Attachment and Separation*, Reite, and Field T (eds), Orlando Academic Press, 1985, USA.

7. Perry B, 'Neurological Development and the Neurophysiology of Trauma', *The Advisor APSAC*, 6:1 and 6:2, 1993.

8. Erikson E H, *Childhood and Society*, Norton, 1950, USA.

9. See 3 above.

10. Maluccio A, Feine E, and Olmstead K, *Permanency Planning for Children: Concepts and methods*, Tavistock, 1986.

11. Kagan R, and Schlosberg S, *Families in Perpetual Crisis*, Norton, 1989, USA.

12. See 3 above.

13. Crittenden P, 'Treatment of Child Abuse and Neglect', *Journal of Human Systems* 2: 3-4, 1991, USA.

14. See 3 above.

15. See 3 above.

16. See 3 above.

17. Hess P M, Proch K O, *Contact: Managing visits to children looked after away from home*, BAAF, 1993.

18. Triseliotis J, *Open Adoption: The evidence examined,* in Adcock M, Kaniuk J, and White R (eds), *Exploring Openness in Adoption,* Significant Publications, 1993.

19. See 1 above.